To Doug Marshall

All the best

Benjamin F. Rathbun
November 1997

Captains B.F. Rathbun & Noank

Benjamin F. Rathbun

Noank Historical Society, Inc.
P.O. Box 9454
Noank, CT 06340

ISBN 0-9659887-0-8
Printed in the U.S.A.

Editor's Comments

The Noank Historical Society, Inc. is honored to be publishing *Captains B. F. Rathbun of Noank* through the generosity of Captain Benjamin F. Rathbun, Jr. Over the years Ben has given to Noank in many ways, among them his lively reminiscences at the Society's meetings. Drawing from these popular programs, Ben presents a wonderful balance of storytelling and Noank history, as entertaining and accurate as any written history can be. Ben has the rare gifts of a vivid memory and the ability to turn an ordinary event into an interesting anecdote. Not many of us who have witnessed extraordinary events like the Hurricane of '38 were disciplined enough to record them for posterity. He has the talent, drive, and perspicacity to make his story an historical treasure.

Although of a specific era and locality, these stories are about relationships as universal and timeless as man. Ben, as a product of that era, exemplifies the pragmatic philosophy of doing without, or making things work. He recalled that during the 1930s Depression, his family was "poor—so poor that we didn't always know if there would be a next meal." But Ben also recalled that he didn't feel poor because other families in Noank were poor, too, and because he was rich in family, community, energy, faith, and education. For both Ben and his contemporaries, the old Victorian Noank Grammar School, with its outhouses in back, enriched them with high educational and personal standards. Noank School and Mrs. Morgan's instruction and discipline proved a good basis for Ben's scholarship and writing.

Influenced by his community and family heritage, Ben is religious to the core but probably would deny it. Although he now doesn't espouse a particular religious persuasion, he, his parents and his children attended church, taught Sunday School, sang in the choir and participated in many church activities. His ethical principles, extraordinary sense of fairness and Christian humanitarianism shine through these adventures of hearty Noank fishermen.

Ben helps us visualize an era when camaraderie among the Noank fisherman, boat builders, and villagers formed an interwoven net of mutual welfare and support. This circle of helpfulness is very present in Ben's stories, from the scholarship given to Ben's father by a Noank family in 1914 to Ben's unstinting work for the Noank Fire District in the 1990s. Ben's stories reveal this special community bond that existed within the Noank village, a bond of cooperation and responsibility, a bond not necessarily based on intimate or social friendships, but a bond to the place, this peninsula of Noank, where interdependent lives were tied to each other and to the sea.

Captain Rathbun, well versed in his profession as a lifelong waterman, is proficient in many intellectual and practical fields. Far from winding down into retirement, he is a busy marine surveyor and member of the Noank Fire District Executive Committee. Ben uses his knowledge and firsthand experience of the fisheries industry to forge a wise policy for the country. In 1986 he was appointed to the National Oceanic and Atmospheric Administration's (NOAA) Sea Grant Review Panel, and was its chairman from 1988–1989. In 1990 he was appointed a member of the National Extension Committee of the Joint Council on Food and Agriculture Sciences, U.S .Department of Agriculture. Currently he serves on the New England Fisheries Management Council. Ben is as conversant and comfortable about cyber space as about the marine world, no easy accomplishment for one who began school in the 30s. He gets a big thrill from mastering the computer and fishing the internet, perhaps similar to the high he described stalking, catching, and landing the regal swordfish when the fishery was done with a hand-thrown harpoon.

Ben's stories delight us with gems of wisdom. For example, at the end of the Noank School story I said, "Why didn't you say that all the class was mad at you?" Ben replied, "Because all of everything never happens." With candor, feeling, lively colloquialisms and insight, he draws a vivid picture of his life on the waterfront and the struggle for a livelihood in Noank, a village very different from today's "gentrified" Noank.

Working with Ben in editing his book was total pleasure for me, since he did all the work. I am grateful to him for his confidence and for this unique opportunity to help preserve this segment of Noank's history.

Mary Chrisman Anderson
Noank, Connecticut, 1996

Note: Pictures are from the Rathbun Family collection unless otherwise noted.

FOREWORD AND AUTHOR'S NOTES

Like many things you end up doing, I did not originally set out to write about some of the experiences and impressions of my youth. As a matter of fact, I had begun working on a book about the local islands and lighthouses and simply ran out of steam. I was mulling over what to attempt next, when the impetus for this hodgepodge of recollections was triggered by finding some of my Dad's diaries while cleaning out my mother's house after she had to be placed in a nursing home. Unfortunately, she had destroyed all but a few of them in a fit of cleaning up but, as luck would have it, among the survivors were his reports of the 1938 and 1944 hurricanes. Thinking that some of my children would be interested in reading his accounts of the two storms, I copied them on my word processor and printed them out. This exercise evoked memories of some other events that took place when I was growing up in a small New England town. With that as an impetus, off I went in an attempt to give my kids a feel, as best as I could, of how it was back then.

I guess it is a normal human impulse to remember your early years as consisting of long periods of bland every-day happenings interspersed with an occasional memorable event. The majority of the unremarkable events are, for the most part, not only impossible to remember accurately, but would be rather boring to read about unless you jazzed them up with fiction. With that in mind, I have avoided including a multitude of the day-to-day trivia in these essays, not only because I wanted to keep as close to the truth as possible, but because my mind usually draws a blank at the minute details of the mundane daily life of 40 or more years ago.

The very first story I wrote was the one about my Dad almost boiling the minister alive on Easter Sunday. It is still my favorite and possibly the best one I have produced and may be due to hearing uncounted repetitions of the tale during the years I spent working for my Dad. He was a great story teller, and given that it was also his favorite tale and he had a captured audience in his charterboat customers, hardly a week went by without listening to him regale them with a performance of the event. The majority of his other stories he related to me while we were chugging at our top speed of 8 knots to and from the fishing grounds. Now don't be misled by the slow boat speed, we went just about everywhere boats go today at 10 to 15 knots; it just took a lot longer. We left in the dark and most of the time we returned in the dark. On many days this was hours after sundown and we would be looking for the kerosene lantern my Mom would hang on a spile at the end of our dock to guide us.

Writing stories for your own pleasure or only to be read by one's family is easy to do but, as I have found out, writing for publication is another ball game. For one thing, when you write for the family it is usually a one-shot affair. You just crank it out and print it; case closed. Writing for publication by others entails the inevitable rewrites and the juxposition of an editor into the creative process. These are certainly necessary, but tend to be tiresome and emotionally disturbing, for the editorial comments and directives are tampering with your deathless prose ramblings in an attempt to make them interesting and saleable to the public. This naturally causes the author to become increasingly cranky and frustrated with the process as the rewrites and minor changes in content mount up, at least within his mind, into what often becomes an almost irresistible impulse to scrap the whole process. I have been fortunate in having a patient and understanding editor in Mary C. Anderson, who has spent uncounted hours going over this collection of anecdotes. I am sure many times she has been more frustrated by my writing, than I have been with her punctuation and grammar corrections; to say nothing about her often unsuccessful attempts to shorten my sometimes overlong sentences. If this book finally turns out to be well received, it will be due in great part to her efforts on its behalf.

Even though I said at the outset that I began writing these stories merely to give to my kids, over the nearly 10 years which have passed since I first began, the project has assumed a larger role in my mind which has transcended the original purpose. It eventually became not only an attempt to record times past and a lifestyle which will never reoccur, but a restatement of some of the values inculcated in me by my parents and particularly by my Dad. A couple of the most worthwhile axioms he taught me long ago were these. No. 1. Even though all of us carry a certain amount of preconceived personal bias into every situation, we should always try to examine every proposal with as open a mind as possible, so that our final decision can be made on its merits, not on emotion, toward advancing the common good. No. 2. It's no sin to be wrong; the sin is in refusing to admit it and thereby failing to learn from your errors. No. 3. Nobody has a monopoly on good ideas and I could often pick up very helpful information and good ideas from my opponents and competitors if, and this was the key, I paid attention. All of this is by way of saying that, while I never matured enough to get around to admitting it when he was alive, I learned a lot of very valuable things from him that have helped me immeasurably throughout life.

The events and people that I have included in this collection of short stories are, to the very best of my ability, as close to the truth as memory and time allow. I have tried neither to diminish nor to enhance the events involved, changed any names or invented fictitious characters, for the actual personalities and facts are interesting enough for me. If they are also interesting to others, so much the better.

Last, but a very long way from being the least, I owe a great debt of gratitude to my long-suffering wife Rosalie, who has put up with being virtually ignored on more nights than I care to calculate while I toiled away at the computer in the next room. Without her patience, forbearance and understanding, I would never have been able to complete the project.

Benjamin F. Rathbun, Jr.
Noank, Connecticut

CONTENTS

Captains B. F. Rathbun of Noank

ANNA R *underway, my dad in cockpit. Islands from left to right; Gates, Ahoy, Quirk, Ram, Fishers Island on horizon. Photographer: Al Haring.*

INTRODUCTION

Captain Benjamin F. Rathbun lives where he has always lived, on the same street overlooking the mouth of the Mystic River, on the east side of the village of Noank. He was shaped by the sea outside his door, which provided his living. Growing up in a small village, attending a small schoolhouse, enduring the "Depression," surviving the 1938 Hurricane and its after-effects, and working for his father are some of the myriad things that shaped his world. In a sense, the events and activities that have made Noank the place it is today have also made Ben the man he is today.

The experiences Ben relates in this book, as well as the stories he passes on, are told with a bias toward "telling it like it was," not dressed up or polished to seem a fitting history. These are stories of a small village as seen by a child, later as a father's son, and finally as a man who faced the world straight-on. This is the world as Ben has encountered it. While humor seems to be a big part of these stories, the sense that life was and is a serious business is never far from the page.

There is a circularity to Ben's life in Noank. As much as he has been shaped by Noank and its events, so too has Noank been influenced by his active participation in its daily dramas. As a waterman, carpenter, husband and father, committee member, board member, and neighbor, Ben has made significant contributions to his world. Those of us fortunate enough to live in Noank with Ben have benefitted from our daily encounters with him.

As you get to know Ben a little better while reading his book, you will come to know the spirit of the man. He is a man who values respect for others, hard work, fair treatment, honesty. He has found meaning in the many events of his time, and has tried to pass these feelings along. If a phrase were needed to describe Ben's message, it could be "Pay attention, you might learn something." He has done this with his life. With this book, he gives us the opportunity to learn something from his "paying attention."

When asked to write an introduction to this book, I was honored and excited. It has been my pleasure and honor to live and work with Ben in Noank. Growing up in Noank with his children, I knew him then as a fisherman and father figure. As an adult, I have served with him as a member of the Noank Fire District Executive Committee. Childhood awe became respect and admiration for a man who has always given of himself. As you read his work and share his experiences and views of the world, you surely will come to respect Captain Ben Rathbun, Waterman, Noank, CT.

Frank J. Socha
Noank, Connecticut 1996

Captain Benjamin F. Rathbun Sr. and wife, Anna, and author at four months old, August 1928.

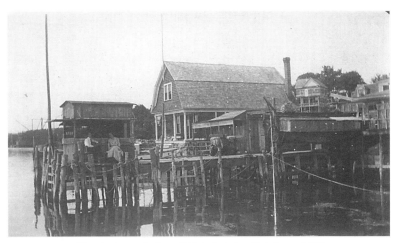

Noank shore, dock and State Lobster Hatchery, 1923.

Dad on ANNA R I. I am at steering wheel, 1 year old, 1929.

Chapter One

Growing Up In Noank

Growing up in a small New England fishing village during what is commonly called The Great Depression was an experience that most any kid living in the same town today would view as a real "bummer." Our lives, by today's standards, were severely restricted, for there was obviously no TV to opiate the mind and insult one's intelligence with idiotic commercials promoting personal items our parents would never dream of mentioning in dinner table conversation. Furthermore, the movie theater, which my Mom had very serious religious reservations about, was three miles away in the next town and we had no family car. Not that we didn't want one, we simply couldn't afford one in those days. An added contribution to this equation was that, like a great many others of their generation, both my parents were inclined toward traditional virtues and were not interested in most of the typical Hollywood films of that era, but felt that good books and small town sociability were a preferred activity. What they would think of most of the current films simply boggles the mind.

However, like so many of our peers in small villages throughout America, we didn't think of it as a "bummer", not for a minute. We didn't have anything to compare our lives to, so we thought it was OK. Sure, times were hard for our parents, but times had always been hard for them as far as we knew; after all, we were only infants when the depression began. If we were missing something as a result of being stuck in a sort of cultural backwater, we fortunately hadn't found out about it yet. At any rate, we were too busy doing the things normal kids our age always do, like getting in trouble at school, fighting during recess and tramping through mud puddles with our good shoes on. We had no time or desire to concern ourselves about poverty, social changes and the other emotional baggage you assume when you grow up.

For one thing, there was the incredibly vivid world of childhood imagination, that was further magnified for us by the wonders of radio. In the same way that my generation, as newlyweds, demolished our budgets to purchase television sets, so our parents did in their time with radios. Radio was, and is today, in an entirely separate class from TV and the movies because, with radio the mind's eye has a range that is limited only by your ability to conjure up images inside your head. With the other mediums, while it may be right there before your eyes: in living color, and a story may be interesting or suspenseful, it can never have the same impact on the brain as a radio production. Who among our generation can ever forget Tom Mix, The Lone Ranger, Bobby Benson, Stella Dallas, Lorenzo Jones and, if you could sneak out of bed to overhear it, there was "I Love a Mystery". Boy, that program could make a little kid run back to bed and put his head under the covers for safety. No wonder we all had nightmares; our brains were running in an overload condition much of the time.

The greater part of the waterfront area, in which our home was located, was in that state of partial decay that characterized most of the small New England fishing villages during the Depression. Actually, it could best be described as a rundown, neglected mess, which means that for a young child it was just terrific. There were plenty of unmowed, overgrown yards for us to prowl around in, many of which were littered with discarded wooden lobster pots which we stacked up to make play houses, forts and hideouts. The shoreline itself was lined with slowly rotting docks that nobody had the money to repair. Looking southwest toward Morgan Point, you could see a number of decaying fishing boats, ranging in size from 20 to 150 feet, hauled up along the shore or in dead storage at Noank Shipyard, with the abandoned 4-masted schooner *ALICE L. PENDLETON* being our unofficial flagship. The junked boats were an irresistible magnet to us and, whenever we could sneak away, we climbed aboard one and took imaginary voyages to the offshore fishing banks that we heard the old-timers talking about. The main difference between us and the present generation was that our play boats were not small plastic replicas of pleasure yachts, but real full-size workboats, and we only needed a little imagination to get underway for Georges Banks in them. So what if the decks were caving in and there was no real motor, we could all make the *kachug kachug* sound of the 2 and 3 cylinder slow speed gasoline engines that the real Noank fishermen used. Attitudes certainly have changed, for if the waterfront was anything like that today, the whole area would be classed as an attractive nuisance by our damage-suit conscious society and fenced off to protect the owners from personal injury litigation.

There was also little in the way of the modern, out in the open, right under the eagle eye of an adult, playground stuff in those days. Oh, our mothers knew where we were-mostly-and generally speaking they expected us to be within shouting distance of home. However, the fact that we were surrounded with so much of what today would be considered "junk" gave us a feeling of independence that you could never achieve in a modern playground. What kid would want to climb on the monkey bars under the baleful stare of an overly protective adult when he could climb through a broken fence and creep through the head-high weeds to a REAL boat that was disintegrating slowly in his neighbor's back lot.

At any rate, although it bore very little resemblance to the social climate and lifestyle facing today's youngster, in its time and place, it was a good environment to grow up in. Besides, it was only the summer visitors' children who fell overboard from the broken-down docks and got themselves drowned. A boy who grew up on the waterfront knew better than to get into a jam where an adult had to rescue him. His mom would really tan his hide if he pulled such a dumb trick. Fall overboard, sure we all did that, it was almost as common an event as walking through a puddle with your Sunday shoes on; but get drowned, my goodness, the possibility never occurred to us, so very few of us ever came close to doing it. Winter or summer, we'd just paddle ashore and go squishing home to get yelled at for being clumsy and careless.

Seriously though, financial prospects were normally rather grim in the Rathbun household, especially in the winter. My Dad was a fisherman and, what with rough weather, poor fish prices and the old converted cat boat he owned not being suitable for winter fishing, he took whatever shore job was available during those months. It was the only way to keep the wolf or the sheriff away from our door. It wouldn't have taken much for them to have gotten in anyway for, like most other Noankers, we never felt it necessary to lock the doors on the ramshackle old house we lived in. There were much better pickings in Mystic or New London.

It is hard to believe today, but in our small corner of the planet, the waterfront area was the least desirable place in which to live. Anybody who was of any importance lived "up-street" (which is what, for some unknown reason, we called the high ground along Pearl and Main Street). We lived on the shore through economic necessity, not by choice, which is rather ironic when you consider the present situation where everyone is clamoring for water-front property at any cost. Although the fact that the entire economy had been in the midst of a crushing depression was a contributing factor, a large part of the reason for the marked lack of enthusiasm for a waterfront home in Noank was the general run-down condition of the entire waterfront area, and our dwelling was certainly no exception to the rule.

My boyhood home is not easy to describe, but here goes. A realtor, with the usual optimism of that calling, would have described it as "needing some work" or a "handyman's special." To be truthful, it needed a whole lot of work and some might even have considered the phrase "beyond reasonable hope of repair" to have been a better description of its appearance. The central part of the structure had been built about 1750 as a post and beam, Cape Cod type cottage. The next eight or nine generations of stubborn Yankees then tacked on a series of ells and additions as the need for more space arose. Why the need for a closet had never even occurred to any of them for nearly 200 years is forever shrouded in mystery.

However, neither its age, nor the lack of a place to hang up clothes out of sight instead of on pegs along the walls, would have been an insurmountable difficulty to my family. Our housing problems were caused by someone who had been dead for nearly a century before I came along. The story, as near as I can determine, is this. Several generations before my grandparents bought the south half of the

Our house about 1921.

Our house, 1923. Note dormers on DeBiasi house in back.

Rathbun home, Riverview Avenue spring 1938. Packing boxes removed from hole in wall to begin repairs. Left side of roof has good shingles.

house, the man who then owned the property, in a well meaning but fuzzy-headed gesture, bequeathed the family homestead to his two sons, to be shared equally by them upon his demise. It would have to be concluded the two brothers did not get along with each other very well, for they eventually divided it into two separate dwelling units and, if you are at all familiar with the layout of a typical Cape Cod style house, there is no possible way a division of that type can work out from the standpoint of livability. A Cape Cod cottage is not designed to be converted into a two family home, especially when you split it left-right starting smack dab in the middle of the front door.

Along with this architectural disaster went the gruesome fact that only one of the siblings was inclined to do any work on his half of the structure. From our vantage point in the present, it is evident that the heirs to the neglected side must have been cut from the same piece of cloth as their sire for, although they continued to rent their half of the property to Charlie, Andrew and Aunt Lizzie Potter, they would neither fix it up or agree to sell it to someone who would. The result of this impasse was of course inevitable. As time extracted its toll, one side maintained some semblance of repair, but the other portion had deteriorated badly. Compounding the whole mess was the fact that, although the breed was extremely stubborn, they were very fecund or maybe just careless. For whatever reason, this breeding frenzy produced a total of 18 part owners, many of whom had very little in common with any of the others, making it virtually impossible to get everyone to agree about selling it to anyone.

The south half where we lived also had a complex history of ownership prior to our arrival, some of which is forever shrouded in mystery. What is known is that Charlie Potter bought 1/7 of it from the estate of Esther Weeks on May 15, 1917 for $114.28 and followed it up on August 11, 1917 by buying 6/7 of it from Richard and Sylvester Weeks, Louela Howell, Bertha Latham, Eleanor Musante and Maud Sweet, presumably for the same price per share, for a grand total of $799.96. He then sold it to my maternal grandparents for $1,000.00 on January 4, 1918, who, in turn, gave it to my Mom and Dad when they got married in 1924. Unfortunately, due to its complex legal status and the shaky state of the Rathbun family finances, the north half continued to deteriorate. Finally, with the invaluable assistance of Robert P. Anderson Sr., my parents finally gained total possession of the house in late June of 1938, just in time for both halves to be seriously damaged by the September 21st hurricane.

In the meantime we lived in the "good" side and, although it had been fixed up as comfortably as my parents could afford, they could do nothing about the other half. After the last tenant, Aunt Lizzie Potter, passed away in the early 1930s, the north half of the house was in such a sorry state of disrepair that there was no possibility that it could be rented again. In fact, when I was about 7 years old, one of the outside walls on the "bad" side simply collapsed during a winter storm. The opening created a severe heating problem on our side, and it was a good thing that, in those days of yore before the corrugated cardboard box came into general use, nearly everything was shipped in wooden "packing boxes" for they were what we used, along with old blankets, to patch up the gaping hole for the rest of the winter. Although packing boxes and blankets do not have a very high "R" factor as insulation, they are a lot better than an open 8 X 12 foot hole in the outside wall of an adjacent room.

Noank was a typical small town of that era and, as such, the local churches had a much greater influence on the daily life of their members than they have today, especially socially. In most cases the social life of an entire village was directly tied to the activities of the most active church, whatever its denomination. A minister or priest who was a good organizer of these events was a valuable asset indeed, and if you were fortunate enough to have one who could read music, sing passably well (especially tenor) play the piano and direct the choir, you hung on to this jewel with all four feet.

My parents attended the local Baptist church not, I would think, through any strong belief in the relative merits of baptism through immersion over other methods, but because they were both musically talented people and the Baptists had the best choir in the area. My mother was an accomplished pianist and a dynamite sight reader. My Dad was a take-charge type of guy with a great sense of humor and soon became choir director. Being closely involved in these secular activities puts you on the inside track, so to speak, and when the janitor's job (they call themselves Sextons these days) became vacant one fall he snatched it up, grateful for any extra income. The job description was straightforward enough: tend the coal furnace, shovel the snow off the walks (only a handful drove to church and if it snowed, getting up the driveway was their problem), clean the Meeting Room and the Sunday School Rooms (now called the "Sanctuary" and the "Christian Education Department") and, perhaps most important of all, ring the bell for services.

Boy, did I love to watch my Dad ring that bell! It was, and still is, a fairly substantial bell for a country church and to start it swinging from a dead stop required all his weight for the first couple of pulls. Once he got it rocking away it wasn't hard to keep it going, but working it up to that point took considerable effort. This would not have been too difficult if simply tolling was all the job required, but the minister, who was a stickler for properly conducted ritual, had decided he preferred a more distinctive dong-dong-pause sequence. The upshot of this edict was my Dad ended up hanging onto the bell rope with all his weight about 50% of the time, a decidedly unacceptable procedure in his view. However, it wasn't long before his experience as a lobsterman, which had accustomed him to handle ropes no matter how fast they were moving or how much strain was on them, came into play and he figured out an easier method.

The bell itself was rung from an ante-room adjacent to a balcony which overhung three sides of the Sanctuary. The ante-room was also the principal passageway to the balconies and had a wide semi-circular stairway leading up to it from the lower level. The stairway was the old fashioned open type with a heavy wooden railing protecting the outside of the platform, which terminated at the head of the stairwell in a six inch square newel post capped with a large mahogany ball. The ball was the key to the success of his "improved" technique for, once the bell had rung the second "dong" and was at the top of its arc, the bell

My Dad with me in sled, 1 year old, 1929.

Noank Baptist Church prior to the steeple fire, August 1938.

rope would be all the way down. At that precise moment, quick as a flash, he would flip a turn over the ball; there would be a muffled creak from the 1 inch manila rope as it stretched under the weight of the half-ton bell and, there it would be, ready to start ringing again when he jumped the turn off the knob. "It's all in catching the bell right at the very top of its arc" he'd say to anyone who happened by. In retrospect, I guess the full significance of "catching the bell right at the very top" was not fully realized by some of those who watched the show every church service. It was another of those deceptively simple moves all natural athletes are capable of and my Dad looked so casual doing it that it was easy to forget he had been in the Army Air Force in WW1, was a crack shot and played both baseball and basketball at the semipro level.

A few years later, after Dad moved on to better things, one of his prior spectators decided to demonstrate how "Benny", as he was known locally, used to ring the bell. Alas, he waited a fraction of a second too long, the 1000 lb. bell had started back down before he flipped the hitch over the knob. There was a shriek of splintering wood as the newel post came ripping out of the floor and shot half way up to the ceiling of the vestibule. This episode definitely ended the use of that technique for all time.

Besides watching my Dad ring the bell, my other favorite pastime was watching the care and feeding of the coal-fired furnace. Anyone who has hand-fired a large, industrial coal furnace knows it is not a simple job to get and maintain a good bed of coals. Sure, the shoveling is hard dirty work, what with the dust and the ashes, but it's still a satisfying job in a peculiar way, if only because, in addition to experience and skill, it takes a certain "feel" to do it right. My Dad had the feel, I guess, because he could make that fire do anything he wanted it to do. If the deacons decided they needed more heat, it was darn soon coming.

Things seemed to go fairly well with the janitor job (sorry, I keep forgetting to call it Sexton) until the lenten season came along; at which time many of the church leaders began to get rather up-tight and fidgety. As nearly every American knows, Lent is the single most important religious event in the Christian calendar, culminating in that holy and joyous day, Easter Sunday. In a rural New England Baptist church in the 1930s and 40s, Easter was truly the highlight of the religious year, with most of the congregation involved in some part of the many services that had been scheduled.

The Sunday School (sorry, I mean the Christian Education Department) was in a turmoil, for it was the end of the year and all the children normally graduated to the next class. For many of us, promotion was more likely to be a desperate attempt by our Sunday School Teachers (now often called Instructors) to get rid of some troublesome pupils, than a measure of our religious fervor. In fact, my class had the dubious distinction of establishing the all-time record for making teachers quit teaching Sunday School. This may appear to the uninitiated as a debatable honor at best but, at that time, we were looked upon by our peers as models of cleverness and duplicity; especially when we could get the more genteel old ladies to burst into tears and run sniffling to the Sunday School superintendent. Now, before you jump to an erroneous conclusion, we weren't actually unruly or noisy, as that would have brought swift retribution from our mothers. Today we probably would be described as "active children", although sneaky or sly might be a better term. Most of our unsociable behavior consisted of making faces behind the teacher's back, furtively passing notes back and forth or drawing cartoons of Bible characters, one of the deacons or, perish the thought, the pastor. My best friend in those days was Arnold Crossman and he was a positive genius at drawing simply outrageous cartoons and these, coupled with our other efforts, so distracted our teacher, dear old Florence Oliver, that she quit teaching Sunday School immediately after our class graduated to the next level.

Along with the promotion ceremony, we had to practice our parts in the Lenten and Easter pageants, which the long suffering teachers coerced the reluctant kids into performing for the congregation. As a typical growing child, I was too painfully shy to actually enjoy standing up in front of an audience, much less attempt to speak my lines without screwing up. To be honest, I really can't remember much about any of the many little playlets we were forced to appear in during my so-called formative years. I suppose, like most of the small traumas you encounter when you are young, my subconscious mind is simply refusing to recall those events.

The adults were even busier than the kids, for they first had to teach their children to sing or speak their parts, and then convince them of the fearful consequences that would result if the child pulled a no-show on them. They also had adult-type roles in these and other productions to prepare for and, most important of all, the church music to perform. Except for the early Puritan era, vocal music has been an important part of a New England Easter service, with the choirs practicing many hours on their anthems and, if you had a top flight group such as we had in our church, you also performed an Easter Cantata, which is actually a longish anthem with several solo parts involved. This was THE MAJOR MUSICAL EVENT of the year and almost all the amateur vocalists were a little nervous about the whole thing. After all, nobody wants to look foolish in front of a Sanctuary filled with your friends and neighbors, especially if you were selected to sing one of the solos.

Easter Sunday was always tough time for Reverend Ernest Wise, for he had to preach not one, but a whole series of his best sermons that would, hopefully, stir the hearts of the faithful. In addition, he had to attempt to lure back into the fold those who had strayed from the rather narrow path that was prescribed for us in those days and last, but by no means least, to attempt to bring to redemption those who were not yet saved from a LIFE OF SIN. This was a tall order for even the most adept preacher to fill. Not only that, in addition to the already described ministerial duties, as a Baptist he was required to officiate over the baptism ceremony. For those readers who are uninformed concerning Christian religious practices it will suffice to say that, unlike other denominations who christen their followers when mere infants, Baptists want their candidates for immersion to be, theoretically at any rate, old enough to have made independent decisions about the matter. Whether this is the case, or whether peer and parental pressure would rank right up there with religious zeal, is probably unimportant. As my Dad often said, it matters not which road you take to heaven, just so long as you get there in the end.

The ability to recruit a sizable class of candidates each year and to successfully immerse them in a solemn and graceful manner without any serious incidents was where a Baptist minister swam or sank, figuratively speaking. It is not without good reason that some of them began to develop a nervous twitch in early spring just thinking about the whole deal. Undoubtedly, more than a few preachers have had nightmares about some sweet, demure young adolescent female suddenly turning into a raging hydrophilic as the minister, after receiving an affirmative answer to his question concerning her belief, gripped her carefully, but firmly, and began to tilt her back until her head was completely under the water. If our pastor had any of these misgivings he kept them well hidden from the congregation. Two weeks before Easter, he announced what was in store for the congregation. We were to have three special programs at the morning service, a Sunday School pageant, the Easter cantata and a baptismal ceremony following the sermon. While certainly not a primary goal, this schedule also made good sense from a business standpoint, for the three events would involve so many families that the participants alone would nearly fill the Meeting Room. With the normally faithful providing a healthy head start, pleasant weather would guarantee a full house and result in a substantial collection when they passed the plates for the "Offering".

Chapter Two

MY DAD AND THE BAPTISM

Although my Dad had taken over the job when the fishing season ended in the late fall of 1936, this was to be the first baptism since my father became janitor, excuse me, I mean the Sexton. I guess he was a little nervous that he might overlook a crucial step or foul up somewhere in the procedure, for he hunted up the old codger who previously held the job and asked him if there were any tricks involved in preparing for the baptism. "There's really nothin to it," he was told. "Jus fill tha tank ta tha top-a-tha upper step'n it'll be OK. Add any more an it'll be ovah tha little ones' heads, an any less water'll cause a problem in gettin tha adults alla tha way undah tha watah. Oh yeah, there's somethin wrong with tha watah heatah too, but there's nothin you kin do about that, so don't worry none about it. The cussed thing jes don't seem ta draw right an even running it all night long hardly gets tha watah warm enough ta keep tha little ones from freezin ta death when they get inta it."

Before going any further it might be a good idea to explain some of the peculiarities of the water system in use at that time. To begin with, there was no city water in Noank in those days and the church, like most everybody else in town, depended on a shallow well. Easter Sunday, being geared to the solar calendar and thus falling on the first Sunday after the first full moon after the vernal equinox, is a spring event and well-water temperature is normally too cold for comfort that time of year, especially if you are a Baptist minister and have to stand in it up to your armpits for a considerable length of time. This had always been the case in colonial days but, about the turn of the century, some philanthropist donated a tiny, well worn, coal-fired water heater to the parish. It was received with mixed emotions for, while the clergy hailed it as a outright godsend, the janitors all cussed it due to its small size compared to the volume of water that had to be heated. Furthermore, the firebox only held coal enough for 3 or 4 hours, which meant the janitor had to feed the little monster every few hours the night before the scheduled event. No wonder they all disliked it. There was a considerable amount of water to heat and, seen through a child's eye, the baptismal tank looked simply immense. As a matter of fact, it actually was quite a bit larger than a normal baptismal tank, being, as near as I can remember, about ten feet long by about six feet wide and, when filled to a depth of four feet, it held nearly 1800 gallons.

It also held a lot of water to fill with a hand-pump. That's right folks, a hand pump was the method used and required several hours of continuous effort at the handle of a big cast-iron force pump permanently piped from the well to the tank. Anyway, the former janitor claimed the heater didn't draw well enough to get a good fire, or so my Dad had been told. He was rather puzzled by this information because the water heater and the main furnace were both connected to the same chimney and the big furnace had plenty of draft. The suction was so strong my Dad often said that you could pull a hippopotamus up the chimney in a 30 knot breeze if you could get one in the flue. With this thought in mind, he began to take apart the 50-year-old smoke pipe between the water heater and the chimney and, sure enough, several of the elbows were almost completely blocked with soot. It only took him a few minutes to remedy that situation by dumping the accumulated coal dust into the ever present ash barrel and the pipe was clear. As soon as he finished reassembling the pipe he lit a fire to see if he had solved the problem. It took off with a roar and I knew from watching that he was really pleased with himself for solving the problem so quickly. "It's probably been plugged up for years," he grumbled. "It's no wonder they couldn't get the water warm enough to satisfy anybody." Unfortunately for later developments, the chimney repair took place only a couple of days before Easter so, although proud as punch with the results, he had neither time or opportunity to let anybody else know about it, for he and my mother were busy as beavers, cleaning and polishing the whole interior of the church. I distinctly remember he was still rather pessimistic about trying to warm all that water with a tiny stove, even after he stoked it, faithfully, every few hours all Saturday night.

Easter morning dawned bright and sunny, practically assuring a fine crowd of the faithful at morning worship. Our entire family was in more than the usual Easter Sunday morning turmoil, what with two boys in two separate playlets and both my parents singing in the choir. Plus my father had to ring the bell and adjust the steam valves to keep the Meeting Room/Sanctuary at the proper temperature for the deacons. By the time the service began, the pews and the balconies were packed solid. The pious, who normally made up the vast majority of the worshipers, were augmented and, in fact, outnumbered by the not so pious who only appeared at Christmas, Easter and funerals. To the great relief of the parents, we kids did passably well in our little pageants, which is not to imply we did great. What it actually means is that nobody screwed up bad enough to panic, start to cry and go running off the stage pleading for "Mommy." The choir performed with commendable skill, my Dad singing the bass solo in the Cantata and my Mom holding down the alto part in the quartet refrain in the anthem. All in all, it was an auspicious start to the day.

Reverend Wise, the minister, who normally was an extremely austere type at best, looked as if he might even smile as he took to the pulpit and began his sermon. He really pulled out all the stops, delivering one of his best attempts at explaining the doctrine of the Resurrection and the many benefits of salvation versus the virtual certitude of eternal damnation for unrepentant backsliders and unbelievers. He would have earned himself a chorus of "Amens" and even a tumultuous round of applause if such a show of approval had been permitted. Even so, it was obvious from his appearance and gestures that he knew he had turned in a stellar performance for his flock. He then raised his arms as a signal for the congregation to rise and announced the hymn to be sung as an entr'acte while the Meeting Room was being prepared for the baptism ceremony. It was a hymn of many verses and he indicated that verses 3 to 5 would be sung as a repeat refrain if they needed more time to get everything ready. I remember, prophetically as it turned out, the chorus began with the words "Just as I am without one plea."

Getting ready was no mean feat and involved a sequence of people movements and scenery changes that would have been worthy of a Broadway production; all of which were coordinated and carried out in what could only be described as a model of 19th century planning. It was actually a little like attending a theater in the round without a blackout to mask the movement of the players and the props. First, the minister retired through a door behind his pulpit to change into one of the lead-hemmed baptismal robes he and all the candidates wore when they entered the tank. The lead weights sewn into the hem were there for a good reason, especially for the female sex, as they were taking no chances the robes might trap air, float up to the surface of the water and expose some sweet young thing's undies to the full view of the minister. Although I never got up the nerve to ask, I always found it rather incongruous that the preacher wore a black robe and the sinners preparing to be ritually cleansed wore white.

We also had an unusual arrangement for the choir at that time, for they sat up in front on the podium facing the congregation. I never learned the reason for this departure from a New England choir's usual position on the rear balcony, but rumor has it that the change had been instituted a few years previously as a form of discipline for an excessive amount of whispering and tittering during a particularly boring sermon. At any rate, they had to sit up there behind a fairly high, solid mahogany rail and maintain some semblance of composure through thick and thin. A minor saving grace being that, when seated, they were only visible to the congregation from the shoulders up. Now, someone who has never sung in a church choir cannot even begin to appreciate the degree of indifference most choir members have to any part of the service not directly connected to THEIR music. The Noank position, being up-front in plain view, virtually eliminated the lip reading, weird facial expressions and gesturing employed by choir members the world over for communication when stationed out of sight in the rear. But ingenuity being the mother of invention, my Dad, his good friend Robert P. Anderson Sr. and several of the other free spirits had developed the art of hand signals and note passing to a high degree. My Dad and Robert Anderson also delighted in transposing the words in the hymns during choir practice, a supposedly harmless enterprise, that backfired one Sunday when they both slipped up and bellowed out "Keep your eye upon the throttle and your hand upon your rail" instead of the other way around.

When you think about the situation, it must have been a tremendous strain on a person's self control to keep a straight face when a particularly funny joke was passed around, or one of the folding wooden chairs began to collapse. An even more extreme tactic, employed only on rare occasions, was to furtively step on the hemline of a nearby member's floor-length black choir robe when everyone stood up to sing; females were the most often targeted, but men would do in a pinch. This could, and many times did, have some very alarming consequences if the seams along the shoulders were a little weak. These goings on, and the other shenanigans, sometimes caused the men in the rear row to get the snickers so bad they would slump down out of their chairs onto the floor and slither out the rear door to the safety of the antechamber. Somewhat like-now you see them, now you don't. How the rest of the gang kept from completely cracking up while all this was going on I'll never know, but it did help to train a whole generation of absolutely inscrutable poker players. After a few years in the choir, Houdini himself couldn't have read your mind using your facial expressions.

Be that as it may, after the departure of the minister, the choir would fold up their chairs, carry them out the southeast side of the rail and down two steps onto the main floor level. Once there, they leaned them up against the outside wall and took seats in the first two rows of pews, which had been blocked off for their use, while continuing to sing along with the rest of the congregation. The six deacons, doubling as stage hands, then went up onto the podium, picked up the pulpit and wrestled it down onto the northwest side of the lower level. The pulpit, made from solid mahogany and weighing at least 200 pounds, was no toy and watching those rather elderly men in their best Sunday suits straining their guts out while trying to look cool, always gave us kids the giggles.

Next came the rail. If you are beginning to get confused by all this, I guess I should mention that the baptismal tank was underneath the floor of the podium behind the rail. The rail, about 15 feet long and at least as heavy as the pulpit, sat on the edge of the platform over-hang and was held in place by a clever system of bolts whose nuts were therefore accessible from the front. When everything went according to plan, meaning when none of the nuts were frozen up and refused to turn, it usually took a couple of the black frocked deacons at least three or four minutes to unbolt everything while the others kept the partially loosened rail from tipping over. When all the bolts were finally free, all six deacons lined up alongside the rail and, at a nod from the elder deacon, heaved it up, struggled down the steps with their awkward burden and carefully leaned it up against the front pews. By this time the congregation and choir were on their third or fourth go-round of verses three to five of "Just as I am, without one plea" and were getting rather bored by the whole affair. However, it gave everyone something to do while the deacons were doing their thing and kept the adults, at least, from squirming around and talking.

With the rail removed, the stage was then cleared of the palm fronds and lilies,

Noank Baptist Church interior. Photo: Noank Historical Society, Inc.

traditionally placed there every Easter. At long last, all systems were now "GO" and the rear third of the podium could finally be rolled back out of the way. I realize the whole set-up sounds somewhat like a cross between a fish story and a fairy tale, but you have to remember the baptismal facilities had been designed and built sometime in the mid to late 1800s when complex mechanical contraptions were all the rage. The identity of the architect who designed the Noank baptismal tank set-up is hidden by the mists of antiquity, but Rube Goldberg would have been really proud of him.

Although I admit I am guessing at its exact size from memory, about an 8X10 foot section of the platform over the tank was supported on each side by a series of small double-flanged steel wheels running on two parallel steel rails that extended under the rear wall, which was framed up in that area to allow the floor to slide beneath the baseboard. Like the pulpit and the rail, this was a very substantial piece of furniture and was moved, with considerable difficulty, by means of a rack and pinion arrangement driven by a big steel crank inserted under the stairs in the rear antechamber. With a couple of the more athletic deacons (who else) manning it, the platform would slowly slide back out of the way. When originally built, it must have seemed like a marvel of engineering to the congregation but, like most gadgetry, as it grew older it was beginning to show signs of a reluctance to perform readily. That Sunday was no exception and it seemed to take more than the usual amount of shoving, tugging and grunting to get it rolling. Finally, with all the customary squeaks and creaks of poorly oiled bearings and overloaded steel wheels running on steel rails, it slowly rumbled back.

This day, however, when it slowly grumbled its way to a stop and the tank was opened to view, there was a major surprise. A wispy, but unmistakable, cloud of steam slowly drifted from the surface of the water and rose ominously toward the ceiling. The choir, seated facing the front, now had their backs to the congregation and we could no longer see their faces, but it is safe to say they were no longer inscrutable. Their musical output suffered as well, for two or three of the more powerful male singers, my Dad among them, completely stopped singing for a moment, leaving the bass section dead in the water, so to speak. Most of them seemed to recover, somewhat, but you could plainly see their shoulders shaking with mirth and their elbows jabbing away at the person next to them.

About then, the minister opened the side door and, hands folded in front with fingers intertwined in the old fashioned prayer form, strode with measured tread to the front of the stage. If he was startled by the little curls of vapor wafting up from the tank he sure didn't show it. His face had the usual mixture of piety and reserve that traditional Protestant ministers of the era seemed to feel befitted their calling, but his eyes were fixed on the choir. Dad told me later, he could feel those eyes boring straight through him as he sat there only eight feet away. The preacher remained standing in that position for what seemed like forever and then slowly raised his arm to show that the singing, mercifully, would stop when the verse in progress was completed and everyone could be seated. I guess both men knew each of them was in serious trouble, but my Dad couldn't very well get up and leave, and the preacher gave no indication of what he intended to do. As a matter of fact he deviated not one iota from his normal format; he gave a short prayer, slowly nodded his head to the choir to tell them to begin the baptismal hymn, turned and mounted the three steps to the top of the podium.

The choir began singing "Oh happy day that fixed my choice" and, as the minister got ready to descend into the tank, his icy composure slipped for a couple of seconds. Without turning his body even a fraction of an inch, he swiveled his head sharply to the left and you could plainly see him clenching his jaw tightly as he glared fiercely right at my Dad. Then, facing straight ahead and with no further sign of emotion on his face, he started down the steps into the tank. It was about a 9 inch drop to the top tread and he put his right foot all the way down in one swift unbroken motion. He stopped right there, with one foot up and the other down and, even over the singing, you could hear him gasp. Although I am quite sure it was against his will, his face underwent a definite change. His nostrils flared, his eyes seemed to protrude even farther than they usually did and his mouth opened slightly as if he were trying to speak; but no words emerged.

He stood there, in that one leg up and the other leg down position, for what seemed like an eternity, as the choir ended the last verse of the hymn and began again at the beginning for lack of anything better to do. He then carefully, with the same determination as before, brought the left leg down into the water until he stood erect and level with both feet on the same step. My Dad had stopped singing completely by then, but the rest of the group were gamely carrying on. Dad said later he was in a quandary. He knew the water was hotter than it should have been, but he was not sure just how hot it actually was. If it were merely uncomfortably warm, as bathwater is sometimes, there would be no reason to panic but, if it were as hot as it seemed to be from looking at the minister, someone ought to call a halt to the ritual. He hated to think about the ultimate consequences of that action but, if the preacher didn't call off the show pretty soon, he supposed he would just have to march up there and drag the stubborn old bird out of the tank to keep him from hurting himself even more seriously.

At this moment Reverend Wise tried to put his right foot down another step. His eyes seemed to glaze over and he was biting his lip, as slowly, ever so slowly, he lowered it toward the second step. It was no good though, he just couldn't make it all the way and he brought it back up alongside the other. He just stood there partly obscured by the curlicues of vapor for a few minutes and it was obvious he was trying to decide what to do next. My Dad, however, had finally made up his mind to act. Like it or not, it was time to take over, so he stood up and began to squeeze his way by the others in the pew. I guess the commotion in the ranks must have penetrated the pain fogged mind of the preacher, because he turned sharply to the left to face the audience and cleared his throat to speak. Dad, halfway out into the aisle by then, froze, the organist suddenly quit playing, the choir slowly straggled off into silence and we all leaned forward to hear what was coming. Again the minister cleared his throat, as if to test his ability to communicate. You could have heard a pin drop on a feather pillow, it was so quiet. Then, in a half whisper, half croak, the words finally came "I find it physically impossible to continue. The ceremony will resume at 7:30 this evening. Thank you for your patience." With that, he turned around, stepped back up onto the stage, went squishing down the steps to the floor level and shuffled out the side door.

Everybody just sat there in a state of shock for a few minutes until the organist began to play the usual closing hymn. In a couple moments one of the older deacons hobbled to the front, gave a very short closing prayer and suddenly it was all over. Dad hurried out back to find out how seriously our spiritual leader had been burned and to offer his profuse apologies for what had happened. Fortunately for both of them, the minister had a fairly low pain threshold and had suffered only a few blisters on his ankles. This welcome news was quickly relayed to the choir, who promptly dissolved into hysterics, for it was just the sort of stunt that many of the menfolks would have pulled off if they had thought they could get away with it. My Dad wasn't smiling, at least not yet, for it took a few days before he could see the humorous aspects of the episode; after all, he was probably going to lose his job because of it.

As soon as Dad got home and changed into some old clothes, he dragged Alex

Cuthbert away from his Easter Sunday dinner and away they went to Walt MacDonald's fish dock in Alex's car to buy ice. Walt fixed him up with ten 50 lb. blocks of ice that they figured should be sufficient to cool the water down to a tolerable temperature. He took me along that afternoon when he went up to church with an oar to mix the water thoroughly. I remember it sure looked funny to see all those ice cakes bobbing around in the baptismal tank. It took all day but, by the time 7:30 P.M. rolled around, the water temperature was down to just under 100 degrees and everything went off smoothly, except the choir seemed to be having trouble maintaining its composure and drew a number of extremely sharp glances from the preacher.

Chapter Three

THE NOVEMBER 1932 GALE

The 1930s, at least as I remember them, had more extremes of weather than we seem to be experiencing today. The winters were definitely colder with much more snow and it was common for the Mystic River to be frozen almost as far down as our dock on Riverview Avenue. In addition to the colder winters, which allowed us to have many weeks of ice skating on the local ponds, nearly every fall we had at least one very severe gale. These were not hurricanes, however, for as best as I can determine, every hurricane which made it up to our latitude since the "Great Gale of September 22, 1815" that practically denuded Fishers Island, had veered out to sea before it reached us. As a matter of fact, until the Great New England Hurricane of September 21, 1938, nobody hereabouts paid much attention to them. Nevertheless, many of these fall storms were really serious events, especially the one that struck during mid November 1932, which actually had higher water and did more dock damage than Hurricane Gloria in 1985. During the 1932 storm, the screened summer-house at the outer end of our dock was washed away, along with most of the dock planks. The loss of the summer house was unfortunate, but the event that makes the 1932 storm stick in my mind after more than 60 years, occurred when my Dad's boat, the *ANNA R*, parted a stern line, got over on top of the dock and stove in a plank just below her waterline.

Although I was only 4 years old at the time, the excitement of the storm and the near loss of my Dad's boat made such an impression on me that it is one of the few events I can remember in some detail from that time in my life. I believe the wind was from the south east at first and the old *ANNA R* was riding the waves easily, bow to the seas. Then, as often happens in a severe storm, the wind suddenly shifted to the south and began to scream. The storm tide, almost even with the decking on the dock before the wind shift, in less than a half hour rose nearly another foot, completely covering the dock. The old dock had been pretty shaky to begin with and the high tide, aided by the 4 to 5 foot waves sweeping across it, soon uprooted most of the planks, making it virtually impossible for my Dad to get to where the boat was now thrashing wildly about in the beam seas.

Dad on ANNA R I before change to raised deck by Eldridge Yard early 1930.

ANNA R I after change to raised deck, taking a charter out for a ride on the Sound, c. 1936.

I have spent over half a century working on or owning a boat which tied up to a Noank dock and there is almost always a window of opportunity to safely move your boat when bad weather is approaching. If you fail to use that opportunity and the weather deteriorates badly you better have good lines with proper chafing gear for then it will be riskier to try to get away from the dock than to stay there and hope for the best. My Dad had missed his chance and was now paying the price for his delay, as I, in turn, have also done on several heart pounding occasions.

By this time, both of my parents were down on the shore watching the boat gyrate about and my brother John and I were peering out at them from the glassed-in porch which used to run along the front of our house. It wasn't long before the manila stern line, which was far from new to begin with, parted at the cleat and the *ANNA R's* port stern quarter went sliding up onto the dock and began to slam down on a spile with every wave. Barring a miracle, there didn't seem to be any way my Dad could save his boat from sinking right before our eyes.

Things looked really bad for the Rathbun family's only source of income, but my Dad, always a man of action until bone cancer struck him down at 58, never hesitated a second. He ran down to the shore and started crawling out along one of the 4X8 stringers, even though he was completely underwater when the waves broke over him. My Mom was crying and pleading with him to come back before he was killed, but, if he heard her, he gave no sign. He appeared to almost lose his grip a couple of times but somehow managed to hang on and get out to the boat, which by then was partly on top of the remains of the dock.

Once aboard, he opened the hatch in the cockpit sole, rammed an old oilcoat into the hole in the bilge with the handle of the deck brush and succeeded in slowing the leak down to a tolerable level. The next step was to get the engine started and try to move away from the dock, both of which had the potential to be very troublesome, to say the least. The old hand-start Lathrop, thank goodness, started after only a couple of bar-overs, but it must have seemed like an eternity to my Dad down there in the cabin trying to get the old mill going while the boat was pounding the daylights out of her bottom every time it slammed down on the dock. As soon as he got the engine started, he jumped out to the controls, threw the engine in gear and nailed the throttle. The boat was still secured by all of the lines except for the broken stern line and, after the first lurch, it fetched up solidly. The Old Man was moving so fast he seemed like a blur to those of us watching him through the driving rain and spray. Grabbing a bait knife from its leather strap on the bulkhead, he leaped forward and slashed through both of the bowlines, bounded aft and cut the remaining stern line and the boat went bumping and banging out of the slip toward the channel. About that time my Mom started screaming "SPRINGLINE, SPRINGLINE" for, in the heat of battle, my Dad had neglected to cut the spring line. Not to worry, the poor old springline never stood a chance; with a 20 foot running start, the 8 ton lobster boat parted the 3/4 inch manila line like a shoestring.

Dad on his first boat (name unknown) at dock.

Our dock after the 1932 storm.

Wreckage of lobster shacks and docks after 1932 storm.

Once clear of the dock, my Dad realized that he was a long ways from being home free. The boat was wallowing in an alarming manner and appeared to be riding much lower in the water than normal. A quick glance through the cabin door confirmed his suspicions; the water was already over the cabin sole and appeared to be rising swiftly. It was obvious that either the oilcoat he had used to plug the leak had been washed away or the continued pounding had smashed another hole in the bottom. In any event, it was a foregone conclusion that the *ANNA R* was swiftly sinking under him and would never remain afloat long enough to reach the shelter of West Cove.

He was just passing Fitzpatrick's dock (now Crowley's) and he knew that the small beach between Fitzpatrick's and Augustus Morgan's (now Giblin's) cottage was the last place on the east side of Noank where he could beach the boat without putting it on the rocks. Swinging the wheel hard to starboard, he gave the old Lathrop full throttle and hoped for the best. There were a few long planks washing around in the shore break and, luckily for him, they made a skid of sorts that enabled the *ANNA R's* bow to slide almost half a boat-length above the water's edge. When the boat had ground to a stop, he slowed the engine down to half speed to keep the boat from slewing broadside and was just standing there wondering what to do next. As he said later, in spite of his obvious troubles he was still having a lucky day for, when he was careening toward the shore with the engine wide open at 660 RPMs, he had seen some men running down the steps leading to the beach, but his whole attention had been riveted on getting the boat ashore before it sunk out from under him.

It turned out that Webb Eldridge and several of his men had heard that my Dad's boat was in trouble and had come over to see if they could be some help. By a great stroke of good fortune, they arrived in time to throw a couple of saw horses and planks under the bilges that kept the boat from falling completely over, thus saving further damage to the hull. After the storm abated, the boatyard gang returned with additional timbers and helped my Dad shore it up securely, including running lines from the top of the mast out to some boulders. The boat was so far up the beach it was out of the reach of anything less than a hurricane, which everyone knew we hadn't experienced in over 117 years. It was therefore decided that it would be best to leave her there while she was being repaired. During the winter my Dad replaced the broken planks, recaulked the seams and, with the help of friends and a spring tide, launched it in April without further damage.

Although not directly connected with this episode, Harve Stein, the distinguished artist and water-color illustrator and his wife Hope were then living in the house I now own on Riverview Avenue. In those days, Harve was still working to establish his reputation and was not as busy as he would have liked to be. During the winter, more to have something to do than anything else, he began painting a watercolor of my Dad working on the boat. As it turned out, Harve soon got busier than he expected and never got around to finishing the painting. When he was moving up to a house on Bayview Avenue (Fontanella's, where the Celottos now live) he gave the unfinished painting to my Dad. My Mom gave it to me when my Dad died and it's now hanging in my stairwell.

ANNA R I ashore by Giblin's after 1932 storm. Morgan's dock at right.
Photo: F. Johnston Collection, Noank Historical Society, Inc.

Chapter Four

MORE CHILDHOOD RECOLLECTIONS

I guess every young person in the world has experienced the dubious pleasure of being lectured to by their parents, or others who have passed the magic age of 50, about how things were different when they were growing up. Inherent in the lecture, which is normally placed in the bored recipient's delete file as soon as the speaker finally stops babbling away, is the tacit implication that somewhere along the line we have lost something important and, yes, even romantic. From my admittedly limited experience, this attitude appears to be especially prevalent among those who grew up in small shoreline communities such as Noank. Now I'm not talking about those misguided zealots who virtually deify the AGE OF SAIL which, by the way, required men to live and work under conditions that very few of us would now be willing to cope with on a daily basis. What I am referring to is the average daily goings-on that took place in our and many other Noank households when I was a pre-teenager. Although I admit that none of us in my generation were forced to do our homework on a slate by the light of a wood fire, there is absolutely no question that the last 60 years have wrought a marked change in the daily life of the average resident in my small corner of New England. Whether life back then was better or worse is a totally subjective individual judgment that I won't even attempt to answer on either a personal level or for the community. In truth, there are just too many pluses and minuses to arrive at a satisfactory answer.

For one thing, in the 30s and early 40s, the U.S. was just beginning to emerge from a shattering economic depression, war clouds were rising over Europe and, for our family, times were very tough financially. As kids, my brother and I didn't know or care that we would have been classed as being barely above the poverty level; we were what we were and, as both my parents maintained a very positive

Brother John (left) and me (right), about 1932.

Family photo taken just prior to 1932 storm. Bungalow on left.

Brother John (left) and me (right) showing birthday tool kit gift from Grandfather, 1936.

outlook, we considered our situation to be normal. While it was not standard fare for all of my young friends, there was more physical work to be done around our house than would be required from most non-farm kids today. This was due to the fact that, from 1938 until about 1945, the majority of our heat during the winter months came from the piles of scrap lumber which my Dad and Mom had salvaged from the remains of docks and buildings washed up in front of our house by the 1938 hurricane. Although we were only 8 and 10 years old when we began what eventually became a 5 year stint, my brother John and I were assigned the job of cutting the longer pieces into fireplace lengths. Later on, we supplemented the depleted woodpile with discarded railroad ties gathered from the railroad embankments and driftwood scavenged from the shores of Ram Island. My Dad was also completely rebuilding our 200 year old home, one room a year as money permitted, so there were plenty of jobs in that department when we managed to catch up with the woodpile.

We had no car in those days, let alone a pickup truck, so all the railroad ties and driftwood had to be brought home by water. We also didn't own an outboard motor, so it was all hand work from start to finish. My brother John and I would row up to either the trestle at Beebe Cove or over to Ram Island and wrestle the railroad ties or driftwood overboard, raft up what we figured we could tow, pile half a boatload of small stuff in the skiff for good measure and start for home with double-banked oars. When we got back to our dock we would drag the heavier logs up the rowboat ramp using block and tackle and, after cutting them into pieces which we could carry between us, lug them up into the back yard. We would then cut these into 2 foot lengths with a 2-man lumberman's saw and split them into sizes my Mom could handle easily. Although getting the wood and towing it home was more like an adventure to us than real work, it sure was a long way from adventure to be hunched over the sawbuck yanking that 5 foot saw back and forth for a couple of hours after school.

In preparation for the summers that my Dad went lobstering, in addition to all the foregoing, there were lobster pot funnels and cages for the glass floats to knit during the winter months. Surprisingly enough, this was something I always liked to help him do. There's actually a certain amount of satisfaction in knitting a small object, such as a pot funnel, that you can finish off in a few minutes but, when my Dad graduated to knitting 100 mesh by 100 mesh sections for an otter trawl he was building, progress became so slow that the bloom was definitely off the rose and it became pure drudgery. Although these jobs may sound somewhat like forced child labor, to the best of my recollection, I don't remember being required to do any of these things as chores, and I don't think we would have been forced to do them if we had really objected. Both my Dad and Mom led by example and it was simply understood that all of us were responsible for helping the family get through some difficult times.

One thing we did have in our household was plenty of live music, for my Dad was church choir director and belonged to a local men's glee club that practiced regularly in one of the member's homes. My Mom sang alto in the choir, played piano for the glee club and, with Harriet Thompson, performed piano duets. I don't know if these are heard often nowadays, but they were an impressive performance to see and hear. We had a long piano bench and the two women would sit there, side by side, and pound out some really great music, with my Mom taking the bass portion and Harriet carrying the soprano or melody part. The two of them had been friends since childhood and had been playing these single-piano duets since they were teenagers so, whenever they got together on a tune that they liked and were thoroughly familiar with, they would really go to town on it. I always looked forward to the glee club rehearsals, because as long as we behaved ourselves, John and I would usually be allowed to stay up until after the music portion was over. My Dad knew it would have been impossible for us kids to go to sleep anyway, what with the noise of the piano and 10 or 12 men singing lustily away downstairs. Although I was unaware for many years that he had an ulterior motive in allowing us to stay up late on these nights, those glee club sessions turned out to have a benefit to me that went far beyond the musical portion. As he explained to me much later, it was his way of educating us in the need for cooperation among equals to benefit the common good. While my Dad, being the choir director, appeared to be nominally in charge of things, there was actually no official leader in the glee club. Each of the members freely contributed comments and suggestions concerning the music and, if there were any prima donnas in the group, they kept their tendencies well out of sight in our home. Actually, my Mom had the best chance at judging the overall quality of a song from her vantage point at the piano and was often the final arbiter they all deferred to when serious musical questions arose.

While I never gave it a thought at the time, with the advantage of hindsight, I now realize my Dad had remarkable musical talent. He never had a lesson in his life but he taught himself the fundamentals of music and 4-part harmony; became quite proficient in writing and transposing pieces for the glee club and the choir; learned to conduct fairly large groups of singers and was invited to be one of the guest soloists on the local radio program "Church of the Air." It was always a big disappointment to him that I, after several years of sporadic piano, violin lessons and a short but futile struggle with the clarinet, had no measurable musical talent for any instrument beyond the Kazoo and only ordinary proficiency at voice. The day he threw up his hands in surrender and declared I was off the hook for any more music lessons, might have been a "downer" for him, but it was like a release from bondage for me.

Another social element in a state of transition during my formative years was the role of the church in our life. My Dad, even though he had no permanent home after the age of 13 and with mostly aged guardians substituting for parents, attended church regularly during the winter months. In summer you had to fish every good day in order to keep from starving to death in the winter. His church attendance was due in great part to the music, with which he was deeply involved, but the bulk of the influence probably came from my mother, who had been raised by a devoutly religious father. Her mother, Mary Peterson Johnson, my maternal grandmother, appeared to go along with the spiritual aspects of their family life, but the major religious instruction definitely came from her father.

My 9th birthday.

My first homemade boat, built from a packing box, 1939.

My family, 1939.

My grandfather, John Johnson, was a kind, gentle man who read his Bible daily and thoroughly believed that every word in it was fact, pure and simple. The Old Testament did indeed cause him some mental stress when it came to answering questions from us kids concerning the accounts of some of the prophets, especially those of Noah and the flood. An Ark that could transport two of every kind of animal on earth might be readily accepted by some Flatlander who had never seen the ocean, but my brother and I were raised in a waterfront environment and we must have really strained his patience when we tried to pin him down on some specific nautical issue. He would try to explain how Noah got around the technical problems of enough space and food supplies, but would eventually shut off debate with his standard retort that "All things are possible to him who has faith."

Later on, when I was a sub-teenager, I tried to engage him in a discussion concerning how he could rationalize the fact that the Bible posited an age for the earth of slightly less than 6000 years since creation but the famous astronomer Hubble claimed light from the recently recognized Island Universes (which we now call Galaxies) had been traveling for many billions of years to reach our eyes. It was probably unfair of me to challenge the old gent with such a question for, ever since the news of Hubble's discovery was announced, the subject was, and in some quarters still remains, a burning question among some fundamentalist Christian sects. Being a typical smart-a-youth, I thought I finally had the old gent stumped but, after some thought, he fell back on an answer that was totally unassailable from his standpoint. "I really don't know what to say on that subject and all I can say is that God sometimes works in wondrous ways that man is not meant to understand." So there.

Surprisingly, my grandfather, although he was one of the most deeply religious persons I have ever known, didn't belong to any of the organized denominations but attended a group known as the Holiness Mission which met in a moderately large room on the second floor of a commercial building in downtown Norwich. The minister there, and formerly at the Bradley Street Mission in New London, was a truly unique character named Charlie Potter who, with his brother Andrew, once occupied the north half of our house and whose sister, Elizabeth (Aunt Lizzie) Potter, lived there until her death in the mid 1930s. Charlie Potter, by the way, was the subject of a story by Theodore Dreiser in his book *TWELVE MEN* during which Dreiser described Noank in a rather uncomplimentary fashion. Charlie, although truly uninterested in accumulating wealth, was a forceful, evangelical type of preacher and, were he living today, would almost certainly have jumped into television and ended up a multi-millionaire in spite of himself. The Holiness Mission itself seems to have encompassed both an evangelical and a missionary aspect and was linked, in some obscure long-forgotten way, to my grandfather's aunt, Violet Peake, who worked at a Lutheran church mission on St. Croix in the Virgin Islands.

When working as a self-consecrated minister, Charlie Potter was a dyed-in-the-wool Bible pounding evangelist who preached his own version of New Testament-based fire and brimstone redemption at the revivals and camp

Charlie Potter and my mom (Anna Rathbun) at Morgan Point, about 1926.

My grandfather (John Johnson) at oars, late 1920s.

Charlie Potter's launch MARTHA.

Martha Potter, 1935.

meetings which were a fixture of religious life in the early part of this century. With his stern visage and steely eyes he must have made a commanding impression on his flock and, from what I gathered from my grandfather, he could be best described as having been a fundamental fundamentalist. This observation is reinforced by the fact that, although Charlie's religious message of salvation was based on the New Testament, his underlying philosophy was deeply rooted in the Old Testament and he even had a portable replica of the Ark of the Covenant which he carried around for display when he preached. Unfortunately, he died when I was about 3 years old so I never actually knew him. After Charlie passed away, my grandfather and several others attempted to keep the small congregation in Norwich alive but, without Charlie's driving force, it slowly faded away and eventually closed.

In addition to being a semi-itinerant preacher, Charlie Potter was a jack of all trades who, among other pursuits, worked at carpentry and took fishing parties from his naphtha launch *MARTHA*. During most of the year he lived in Norwich, but sometime in the early 1900s, he bought the narrow plot of land where my home is today. One winter, without consulting his wife Martha about the design or any of the interior details, he had Sam Patterson build a house on the lot as a sort of surprise. Unfortunately Martha, probably because he went ahead without any input whatsoever from her, claimed she hated the house and absolutely, positively refused to set foot in it again after the first summer. This setback would have been the end of homebuilding and maybe even the marriage for most men, but Charlie was built of sterner stock than that; besides divorce was unthinkable for a man of his faith. If she wouldn't live in a 22 ft wide, 2-story house, built on a 27 ft wide lot, he'd just try something else. Old Charlie was either an eternal optimist or a stubborn, block-headed Yankee for, moving right along, he next bought a used steamship cabin about 18 by 18 feet in size from the Palmer Shipyard, again without bothering to consult his wife. It was then loaded onto a shipyard crane-barge, towed over to the property and placed on the water side of the gravel right of way, which later became the present Riverview Avenue. Fortunately for both of them, Mrs. Potter liked the cabin a lot, so Charlie was finally off the hook as far as a summer home in Noank was concerned.

Charlie, however, had only begun, for the ship's cabin formed a nucleus which slowly grew into a conglomeration of additions and porches that the Reverend Potter tacked on every now and then. With the right of way on one side and the water only a few feet away, the only way he could enlarge the building was to drive some spiles and build out over the water. Luckily for Charlie, the concept of coastal zoning was almost 50 years in the future, for the initial ship's cabin eventually became a 4 or 5 room house that was always referred to as the Bungalow.

Nowadays, we take an adequate supply of fresh water for granted, but up until the 1960s all Noank homes depended on either cisterns or wells for water and it was obviously impractical to dig a well or build a conventional cistern beneath the Bungalow. Charlie simply took the concept of the old time rain-barrel to the max and bought four huge oak hogsheads from the Palmolive Corporation and

Bungalow in 1905. House later owned by Rathbuns on upper left.
Private dirt road is now Riverview Avenue.

Bungalow at its greatest extension, about 1928.

Bungalow and dock shack, about 1928. Riverview Avenue.

put two of them on either side of the building under the downspouts. The barrels were really impressive, standing about 6 feet high, and had originally held over 500 gallons of the palm oil that formed the basis for the well known soap. The other end of the plumbing system, namely the discharge side, was simplicity itself, having no moving parts and leading directly down into the river, as it then did in almost all the other homes along the Noank shoreline. Only the tourists were so bold as to swim in the river using the overhand stroke or, worse still, the Australian crawl with their face in the water. For rather obvious reasons, we natives prudently learned from our parents to keep our face out of the water so we could keep a sharp lookout ahead for Floaters and learned to swim using the breast stroke.

After Charlie died, the Bungalow was taken over by his daughter and son-in-law, Elizabeth and Byron Whitney, who came here every summer until the Bungalow was smashed into kindling wood by the September 1938 hurricane. Byron Whitney worked in New York City for a well known businessman named Bernard McFadden, who was another one of those unsung pioneers that were way ahead of their time. Although hardly remembered today, Bernard McFadden was the health and fitness guru of the 1920s and 30s and promoted a number of what were then controversial ideas, many of which are now well accepted. These included the advice that exercise and fresh air are good for you; weight training helps to build up stamina; light exercise with Indian clubs and fencing promote dexterity; a bicycle is a better means of city transportation than an automobile; and smoking is very, very bad for your health. He also espoused several ideas which were definitely unconventional, especially in the "Flapper" age, such as recommending that everyone should take an air bath in the nude after bathing to let your skin breathe. Surprisingly, McFadden also claimed that, while he felt sunlight on the nude body was good for you in moderation, you should definitely not overexpose yourself, as it would then damage the skin cells.

Even more outlandish, then and today, was McFadden's interest in what was called the "Human Aura." This was a concept somewhat akin to the Kirilian type photography that was written up in a couple of the quasi-scientific magazines during the 1970s and 1980s. The little I know about this exotic subject came from two books, one in English and the other in German, both of which were published in Europe during the late 1880s. These had been salvaged from the debris of the Bungalow after the 1938 hurricane and, somehow or other, ended up in our attic along with some Indian clubs and fencing foils belonging to Mr. Whitney. The books, which I came across when I was about 13, had originally been the property of McFadden and both the flyleaves and the margins of many of the pages were filled with annotations and comments in his distinctive handwriting. I am being totally serious when I state the theory propounded in the two books was that there existed a weak, but observable, aura which emanated from the male and female human body under certain conditions and which could sometimes be photographed.

As described in the books, the main focus of the supposed rays was centered on the primary and secondary sexual organs of the body and, at least in the books, only appeared to take place between subjects of the opposite sex. The other conditions absolutely required for possible observation of the phenomena included the fact that both of the participants had to be totally unclothed, stand facing each other about 3 or 4 feet apart and there had to be total darkness during the course of the experiment. Unfortunately, I now realize there was a flaw in the protocols which would have made any results scientifically invalid today, for the books didn't specify if the two subjects had to undress in the dark or were able to see each other in the nude before the gas lights were turned out. This glaring omission would conceivably skew the data and make its appraisal unreliable.

Being a normal teenager, I freely admit the purported presence of the human aura was of minor interest to me when I first discovered the books. What originally commanded my undivided attention were the anatomically graphic male and female nude drawings showing the vee shaped rays spreading out from the tips of the breasts and the sex organs in the groins of the subjects. After thoroughly digesting every word in the English language volume and poring over the many colored illustrations in both, my curiosity was certainly aroused, both scientifically and otherwise. I therefore began to scheme how I could investigate the possibility of viewing and photographing the human aura myself. However, like any foray into uncharted territory, serious decisions had to be made and several major obstacles overcome before there could be any hope of bringing my fantasy to fruition. The first of which was to decide if I wanted to be a participant or a cool, calm, dispassionate, scientific-type observer. I thought about this for a few days and finally decided that, while being a subject definitely had great appeal, the credit for any success would go to the Scientist who recorded the observations, made the photos and published the results.

Secondly, although I was fairly confident another male could easily be found, there was going to be plenty of difficulty recruiting a suitable female subject. Because all of the people shown in the illustrations were well developed, both physically and sexually, I naturally assumed this was a primary requirement for an aura to occur and, while I couldn't do much about my own immature sexual attributes, I figured that one out of two would be the minimum needed for any chance at success. I therefore had to find a sexually mature girl who, not only would be willing to strip down for us, but who I could trust to keep her mouth shut about our research project, a pretty tall order in anyone's book. I must admit, by virtue of the Noank Grammar School's student grapevine, I had heard of several girls who had supposedly taken their clothes off (and more) for some of the guys, but they were so flat chested and gangly I doubted any of them would possess even a weak aura.

Lastly, and most difficult of all to pull off, I would have to figure out how to sneak a girl and the other guy up to my room without my parents being aware of the scheme and fouling the whole thing up by bursting in on us at a critical point. I could just imagine myself standing there in the glare with my clipboard in my hand (you were expecting something else?) and stammering, "Gee Whiz Ma, it's not what you think at all. This is serious business. We're doing a tightly controlled laboratory experiment in here and you've just screwed it up by turning on the lights. Now we'll have to start all over again from the beginning." Uh Huh! I don't know about you but, somehow or other, I don't think my mother would have swallowed that line of reasoning. Let alone the fact we would have had two, and maybe even three, nude teenagers in my room, at least two of whom would undoubtedly have been visibly aroused. Make no mistake, the consequences of my Mom finding us out were truly staggering and I just kept putting off starting the project until I could decide how I could overcome most of the problems.

Alas, my chance for enduring fame and the possibility of a Nobel prize went down the drain for lack of guts, and I finally concluded the grave risk of premature disclosure far outweighed any potential gains. However, I think there is a very strong possibility that someday someone will prove the theory of a human aura is, in some respects, at least partly correct. After all, if you place two nude, attractive, healthy young people of the opposite sex four feet apart in a dark room, you can't convince me there isn't some sort of life-force emanating from certain parts of their anatomy. Perhaps, in this more enlightened age, some intrepid young graduate student at one of our universities, armed with the latest forms of instrumentation, will renew the quest into an intriguing area which I feel has been neglected far too long. As a matter of fact, I'd be glad to serve as a consultant on the project and even as a backup if the need for one ever arose. Seriously though, I wish I still had the books today as they undoubtedly would be collectors items but, sad to say, my Mom came across the hiding place under my mattress while she was doing spring house cleaning and they vanished permanently, probably into the fireplace if she ran true to form. All I know is she said, "I found those two BOOKS under your mattress and I took CARE of them to keep you from getting any more bad ideas than you already have."

Bungalow after 1932 storm. Elizabeth Potter Whitney (left) and Martha Potter (right).

Chapter Five

THE HURRICANE
OF SEPTEMBER 21, 1938

Copied verbatim from the diary of B. F. Rathbun Sr.
(The words enclosed in parenthesis are mine)

September 21, 1938

Threatening weather. Anna went to Norwich to see her mother. Called Lonny (Porritt) up and told him not to come fishing because the weather looked bad and there was a hurricane down off Hatteras. The wind started to blow strong right after dinner. We moved the row boats to what we thought was a safe place, some against Miss. Jones house and some on top of a lobster car. I left our good one on the cement (ramp at the State Lobster Hatchery) hoping to be able to get off to my boat the *ANNA R* which was at her stake.

Al Haring's boat (the *ADA MAY)* pulled the stake up and came ashore at Waylan Morgan's. I jumped aboard as she went by the rocks and threw a line to Hadley Fitch, Bill Banks and Ray Littlefield. I got the engine going and Bill Banks and I took the *ADA MAY* around to Webster Eldridge's where Al was waiting. Came home and changed my clothes and went up to school with Alex Cuthbert to get the children. Trees were falling by this time so I took Franklin & John over to Halstead Brown's. The hurricane had struck in full force by this time so I remained there with the boys until the wind shifted south; then Halstead, Raymond Coon & I went out to see if we could help anyone. The village was a wreck and the roads almost impassable but we managed to get down to the boatyard (where Ford's Lobsters is today) in time to see the *ANNA R* start up the Mystic River. I saw the old house was still standing completely surrounded by wreckage. The entire east shorefront changed, all the docks gone with a few piles left. I went back with Halstead to watch the *ANNA R* but the lower road by Eugene McDonald's store (on Front Street) was flooded and impassable with big trees. I then went up to Helen's (Halstead Brown's wife and my Dad's cousin) to let them see the havoc wrought by the storm; we watched the *ANNA R* go up the river right over Six Penny Island. The railroad tracks were submerged. I went home and soon Halstead came to help me patch up the skylight and the windows.

I then returned to Helen's and myself and the boys spent the night there.

Early in the morning we came home and had some breakfast then I started out in search of the *ANNA R*. I walked the railroad tracks to Mystic thence to Mason's Island where I found the *ANNA R* half full of water. She struck a ledge and pounded all night. I pumped for three hours and floated her but was not able to get the engine going so I had to leave her tied up to a dock owned by a Mr. Lee of Hartford. I saw Anna and the boys across the river but could not hear them. After exhausting all means of saving the boat I took Mr. Lee's rowboat and loaded it with tackle etc. from the boat and started for Noank. I had a hard pull but I finally made out a flashlight near our house and I called for a light as all the village was in darkness. It was Dr. Roland Hill, Halstead & Ivan Crossman looking for me. They helped me unload the boat and after a hasty meal I slept on the couch in the living room as the beds were soaking wet. Anna had taken the boys to Norwich again. She came down in the morning alone and we started to clean up and pick up and put in the broken windows etc. We both slept in the living room that night. I slept on the army cot and she on the couch.

I started patching the roof and recovering the garage roof. I got another load from the *ANNA R*; she had finally sunk. On the 25th Gladden Baker, Nick Carter, Lonny Porritt and Chuck Tuttle came down and after much work we were able to float the *ANNA R*. Ashby Anderson & his brother William towed the ANNA R to Noank where we ran her up on the beach at Wildes Boat Yard, now Ford's Lobsters. There were no marine railways so that was the best we could do. I pumped her three times during the night and the next day Ernest Francke & I got the boat up a little higher where she remained until the 9th day of October when Gladden Baker, Ed Dennison, George Munsick, Doc Rollins and two men sent by Art Warner were finally successful in getting the boat on rollers and above the high water mark. We have had very good weather since the hurricane and have been able to do a lot of work on the house. I am putting roofing paper on the old part of the house over the ell and shed. Anna helping, also the boys.

Our house, Sept. 22, 1938, the day after the 1938 Hurricane.

October 10, 1938

Beautiful day and weather. Took shingles off the old shed getting ready to put roofing paper on. Anna is helping me a lot. Mrs. Townsend came down with some canned goods for us. We are trying to weatherproof the house on the roofs before cold weather.

Our house, Sept. 22, 1938, showing wreckage of boats and docks piled in front.

October 11, 1938

Fine day. Worked on the roof Anna helping. Boys also helped to pull nails.

October 12, 1938

Beautiful day except for haze. Went out with Max Langworthy, along with G. Baker, Munsick, Art Warner. Did not catch any blues. Grandma and Grandpa down. Grandma's first view of the hurricane damage.

October 13, 1938

Still on the roof putting paper on the ell and shed. We intend to make a new kitchen out in the ell and a shop for myself out of the old summer kitchen. Anna is helping on the roof.

October 14, 1938

We are trying to do a good job on the two roofs. Anna went to Fidelis tonight. No street lights as yet.

October 15, 1938

Still working on the roof. Slow work for two persons. Anna climbs up and is a great help to me.

Excerpts October 16-October 25

10/16—Back on the roof after helping move the *ANNA R* to her winter resting place.

10/18—Finished the roof today and started to clean up the Hatchery dock for the wood.

10/19—Worked all day on the dock and got nearly 2/3 of it apart and up in the yard. Hadley Fitch helping and the boys carrying wood.

10/25—Fixed the sink drain to the shore.

November 14, 1938
The Red Cross investigator called today.

December 6, 1938
Raining in the morning. Went to Red Cross with Elmer Davis to sign contract to fix boat ($184.00) Raymond Ledward for engine ($73.00).

December 15, 1938
Have not received my contracts from the Red Cross as yet.

Our side yard, Sept. 22, 1938, John (left) and me (right).
Lobster car (foreground) is from the State Lobster Hatchery destroyed in the Hurricane.

Chapter Six

THE **1938** HURRICANE
AS I REMEMBER IT

The hurricane of Sept 21, 1938 was without question the most memorable event in my formative years. This includes not only scaring the living daylights out of me while it was taking place, but the fact that it had a serious financial impact on my family which drastically altered our lifestyle for several years afterwards. Memories of the storm and its aftermath are still etched deeply in my mind, even after more than 50 years have passed. The decaying docks and buildings lining the shore in front of our house were swept away. Our home sustained serious damage to the roof, windows and interior and my Dad's boat, while it managed to survive destruction, was badly chewed up and eventually sank. Like most New Englanders during those depression years, my parents only had fire insurance for our home and no insurance whatsoever on the boat, so it was up to them to pay for the repairs to both. With only minimal savings to fall back on and next to no assistance from the Red Cross because my Dad refused to stoop to the groveling and whining which seemed to be the only way to get the local board to provide help, my Dad and Mom really scrimped to buy the necessary materials and had to do nearly all the work themselves. Adding to this financial drain was the reality that a fisherman without a boat is unemployed, so it was all out-go and virtually no income for the Rathbun family that winter. On the bright side, we saved on heating costs by burning the remains of the docks and boats which were piled in front of our house clear up to the bottom of the front windows.

I'll begin with a little background. Because we didn't own a car, my Aunt Katherine had driven down from Norwich the preceding day and picked up my mother so she could visit my grandmother Johnson who was just recovering from a mild heart attack. When the New London Day was delivered that afternoon it reported there was a hurricane off the coast just below Cape Hatteras so, after we had our supper, my Dad tuned our new Sears and Roebuck superheterodyne radio to WTIC to get the Travelers Insurance Company's evening weather report. The announcer casually mentioned that the hurricane was expected to stay well offshore, as they had always done since the early 1800s, but we should expect gale force winds and rain tomorrow morning as it passed by. My Dad immediately got on the phone to cancel his fishing charter for the following day and then my brother John and I helped him haul both of our rowboats ashore. We dragged the old one across the road onto Miss Jones' front lawn and placed the good one upside down on top of a lobster car between the State Lobster Hatchery and the Whitney's Bungalow which, as has been previously mentioned, perched half on the shore and half over the water supported by piles. Pulling the rowboats out of the water was standard procedure when bad weather was forecast and, up until then, they had remained well above any danger.

My Dad's boat, the *ANNA R*, was already tied to her stake across the channel with a new 8-inch manila headfast from Sears and Roebuck which both John and I had helped my Dad prepare properly. This consisted of *Worming* between the strands with tarred trawl runner, Parceling (wrapping) it with strips of burlap secured with manila marline and then serving it tightly with new potwarp for chafing gear. Although it's seldom heard nowadays, the old mariner's rhyme for the procedure goes like this: *Worm and parcel with the lay, turn and serve the other way.* At any rate, it was blowing a gale and raining hard when we got up the next morning so John and I put on our raincoats, crammed the *Souwester* rain-hats down over our ears and trudged up the hill to the old Noank School, he to 2nd grade with Miss. Ethel P. Holman and I to 4th grade and Mrs. Hattie Fitch.

The morning passed, as best as I can remember, without any really noteworthy events but, as lunchtime approached, the noise from the wind was beginning to drown out the teacher. Although I was only 10 years old at the time, you don't grow up as a fisherman's son in a New England coastal village without becoming closely attuned to the weather. I suspect all of us knew something out of the ordinary was taking place, especially when Mrs. Fitch announced that no students would be allowed to go home for lunch unless they were accompanied by a parent. We were still digesting this startling piece of information when my Dad burst through the door of the schoolroom and announced to Mrs. Fitch, "I've come for my son." He stood there in the doorway with his Black Diamond foul weather gear streaming water onto the oiled pine floors and the deadly serious expression on his face made it instantly clear he was not asking her permission. He looked over the classroom, pointed his forefinger at me and said in a voice that was an obvious command, "Franklin, get your coat, leave your books here, come on, times a-wastin!" He already had my brother John in tow and in less than 10 seconds we were out in the hall and he was helping us button our raincoats tightly.

Although the wind had seemed loud in the classroom, nothing had prepared me for the noise that engulfed us when my Dad forced the door open and we stepped out into the schoolyard. Like many New England villages, Noank's streets were lined with large elm trees and the roar of the hurricane force winds in them was absolutely stunning. By the time my Dad took us out of school, the gusts were being recorded at well over 125 MPH and even someone who has been outdoors in a full gale would be hard put to appreciate how it feels and sounds when the wind increases beyond that and reaches the 150 to 175 MPH reported at the height of the hurricane. The pressure of the wind on you increases exponentially and your whole being is immersed in a howling, vibrating universe that imparts an almost nightmarish sensation, especially to a 10 year old boy. The roar of the wind through the wildly gyrating treetops was like a physical blow to my ears. As a matter of fact, the only event in my experience which even begins to approach the sound pressure of a category #4 hurricane is to be seated at trackside during a stock car race. It's no wonder that Alan Villiers, in *The Way of a Ship*, probably the most readable book about squareriggers, writes of "the roar of the gale" in almost awed terms.

As we went out the door, my Dad grabbed each of us by the hand and the three of us staggered and stumbled across the playground towards the front gate. The hurricane force wind was coming from the southeast at right angles to our course and several times all three of us were blown to the ground in a heap. It was nearly impossible to speak, for the wind literally took our breath away and we could only make headway one step at a time as we struggled toward the gate. The gravel playground under our feet was covered with a thick blanket of leaves and small branches rolling and tumbling across the yard at great speed before piling up against the west fence. Just as we reached the gate, several of the large elm trees lining Main Street came crashing to the ground before our eyes and it was obvious there was no longer any possibility of getting to our home on Riverview Avenue without grave danger to our lives. My Dad hurried us out the gate and around to the right onto Ward Avenue where the chain link fence and schoolhouse made enough of a lee to keep us from being injured by the sizable tree limbs that were now hurtling through the air with alarming frequency. The three of us struggled up the rise where the firehouse is today and in a few yards we were able to go down into Halstead Brown's back lot.

Thankfully, it was slightly sheltered in the lee of the houses on Church Street and, while the wind was still roaring away overhead, it was muffled somewhat and seemed to be a little less threatening. When we got to Halstead's house, my Dad didn't bother to knock, he just hustled us in the Brown's back door and, after taking off our wet raincoats, put us on the parlor couch and told us in no uncertain terms to stay put. He then spun the sofa completely around so we were facing the wall and the high back was protecting us from anything that might crash through the front of the house. He ordered both of us to keep our heads DOWN below the back of the couch no matter what happened and went upstairs to help Halstead board up some broken windows. Both John and I were still in a state of shock from our trip from school, and my Dad's stern demeanor and explicit instructions left absolutely no doubt in my mind that the danger was far from over.

The storm was now at its height; the house was shaking and vibrating violently in the gusts and every so often there would be a crash as a branch shattered another one of the front windows. It seemed to me our world was coming to an end but, end or not, neither of us had any inclination whatsoever to disobey my Dad's instructions. Shortly after we had scrunched down on the couch, Raymond

Coon, whose fishmarket was situated on the Town Dock, came bursting in through the kitchen door, soaking wet and nearly hysterical. "The waterfront's all gone," he blurted out, tears streaming down his face. "My fishmarket's been washed away and the docks are all piled up along the shore. Everything I've worked for all these years has been destroyed, and I'm ruined, completely ruined." Dad and Halstead sat him down in a chair and my Dad told him sternly, "There's no time to cry about it now Ray, we've got to get some of these broken windows boarded up to keep the rain from ruining the wallpaper and the rugs. We'll figure out what to do about everything else if we can manage to get through the hurricane without being killed." The lecture seemed to settle Ray down a bit for he heaved himself to his feet and the three of them forced their way out the kitchen door on the Church Street side and proceeded to nail plywood over the outside of not only the broken windows, but all the unbroken ones that they could get to under the circumstances.

In the meantime, my brother John and I were kept under the stern eye of Halstead's wife Helen, who my Dad had delegated to make doubly sure we would not move from the couch. If we had to Go that was just tough luck. We could either hang on or wet our pants, but we had to stay right where we were. We were too scared to argue anyway, for the gusts were coming even closer together, and were now shaking the house so violently it seemed like it wouldn't be long before the building would be blown apart and we would all be done for. However, no storm lasts forever and, after what felt like an eternity, it became apparent the gusts were now getting further apart and the wind was slowly, but surely, beginning to diminish. About this time, Dad and Halstead came in and told us they thought the worst was over, so they were going out to see what was left of the village. Dad gave John and me permission to leave the shelter of our couch and, after Helen gave us jelly sandwiches and a glass of milk apiece, we busied ourselves peeking out the salt encrusted windows to see what was going on outside. By then the rain had almost stopped and little glimmers of sunshine were beginning to show through the scudding clouds. Unfortunately, there was little to be seen from inside the house, for everywhere we looked our view was obscured by the trees that had fallen across Church Street.

After awhile, the two men came clumping in with the news that our old house, although still completely surrounded by water, looked to have survived the storm fairly well. However, my Dad's boat, which we depended on for our income, had finally pulled the headfast over the top of the spiles and, while they watched helplessly from the shore, was even now drifting up the river. John and I were clamoring to get out and see things for ourselves, so my Dad gave in and led us through the maze of fallen elm trees to the Baptist churchyard at the top of the hill.

What a shock that was! There was no longer any roof or a steeple on the church; they were lying in pieces in the parking lot. We had to worm our way through the twisted rafters, which completely covered the space between the church and Scroggin's fence, to get a view of the river. The wind was still blowing a howling gale from the southwest under a nearly clear sky but, after experiencing 175 mile gusts only an hour before, it felt comparably calm. It sure was a strange sight. The air on the hill where we stood was clear and dry but, peering down towards the waterfront, the air was so full of spume it seemed to be misting. Even today, the memory of those huge waves rolling up the bay is fixed in my brain, for Noank harbor looked like a surfing video from Hawaii. Only about three feet of Ram Island was showing above water and the seas, which I estimate to have been about 12 to 15 feet high, were breaking on the rocks at the end of Masons Island with force enough to send sheets of spray high into the air, where the wind carried it at least a half mile towards Mystic. Sixpenny Island was completely under water and we could just make out the shape of my Dad's boat as it drifted completely across the island and disappeared into the mists.

We worked our way through the remainder of what, only a few hours before, had been the roof of our family church and, once we reached Main Street, the rest of the route down to our house on Riverview Avenue was relatively easy. By the time we got there the water had gone down a little and, although the waves were still dashing up against the front of the house, we could get to the landward side without wading. Most of our back door on the south side was missing and the opening was nearly blocked by the remains of the State Lobster Hatchery dock which had crushed it. My Dad dragged some of the timbers out of the way and we managed to squeeze through the opening to enter the house. When we finally got inside, the full import of the force of the hurricane was plainly evident, for the old place was shuddering from the wreckage being battered against the front by the waves. Boom, then a short pause, then another sickening blow would come, as pieces of dock and wrecked boats slammed into the house every couple of seconds. Things were a soggy mess in every room, for the chimney had been blown off level with the roof and the bricks had crashed down through the skylight into my bedroom. Not only that, most of the shingles on the waterfront side of the roof had been torn off and all of the windows on that side had been smashed in. The result was that water was still pouring through the ceilings on the first floor and nearly everything inside the house was soaked with a combination of salt and fresh water.

My Dad was not sure the front wall of our home would survive the continual pounding so we only tarried long enough to check on my German Shepherd dog, Pal, who had been shut up in the kitchen all during the storm and was extremely glad to see us. I wanted to take him back to the Brown's with us but Dad refused, for Pal was death on cats and Halstead had at least 6 or 7 of them. However, we managed to find a couple of dry jackets, made Pal a bed by the stove, put out some food and water for him and, with great misgivings, left him there for the night. I think we were all glad to get out of the house, for the waves were still bashing the wreckage against the front of the house every couple of seconds, and I know my Dad was getting increasingly concerned the house might collapse on top of us. Anyway, there was nothing more we could do, so we walked back up to the Brown's, hoping the old place would still be standing the next morning.

I don't remember much about the night, but in the morning Dad took us back to our home which, surprisingly, had come through the night OK. After making us breakfast on the kerosene stove in the laundry, he told us to keep an eye on the house and try to clean up some of the mess, for we were going to be on our own that day. He had to see if he could find the *ANNA R* and, if by some stroke of good fortune it was still afloat, bring it back to Noank. In retrospect, it is not only a tribute to his confidence in the ability of two boys, ages 8 and 10, to be left alone all day and given the responsibility of keeping an eye on what was left of our home, but indicates just how desperate he felt our situation really was. However, if you did that today and the State found out about it, they would probably declare you an unfit parent and take your kids away from you.

In spite of our tender age, John and I both understood how critical the boat was to the financial well-being of our family and would have been surprised if my Dad hadn't set out to try to find it. However, as for cleaning up the mess, we were still rather dazed by all the events of the past 24 hours and we spent the morning just messing aimlessly about in the wreckage. About 10 o'clock, my Mother and my Aunt Katherine came running down the street, having just driven down from Norwich in a frantic state after hearing over the radio that Noank had been washed out to sea and many of the residents had been drowned. The two of them had a pretty harrowing trip on the way down, for the police in Norwich had blocked the highway and tried to make them turn back. Even under normal conditions, my Mom was a determined woman with cat-like reflexes and she wasn't about to let some city cop keep her from finding out if her family was still alive. She thanked him politely, jammed the Ford into first gear and took off around the barrier by driving over someone's lawn. They had to use that tactic many times on the way down, plowing through yards and over fields in second gear while wending their way around all the fallen trees and downed power lines blocking many of the roads, including access to Noank village. After a tearful reunion, at least on their part, and a look at the mess inside the house they decided it was no place for a couple of small kids to stay and packed us up to return with them to Norwich.

There were, however, a couple of problems. How was my Dad making out in his search for the *ANNA R*, and could we find him to let him know my Mom was taking us back to Norwich. She left him a note on the kitchen table, but she was also very concerned about the boat and, after walking back to the car, we set off towards Mystic. It was tough going, with barely room for my Mom to worm the Ford through the branches of the trees which had fallen across the road. We managed to get to West Mystic and drove down toward Willow Point until we were blocked by debris that had been washed into the road. We got out and walked the rest of the way down to the shore at Mystic Shipyard, where we could see the *ANNA R* across the river next to a dock on Masons Island. It took a lot of waving to get my Dad's attention, but he eventually saw the four of us there and he and my Mom tried in vain to understand what the other was yelling about. It was no use. The noise of the wind and the water was too much to overcome and, after a lot of fruitless shouting, pointing and gesturing by both parties, my Mom gave up the effort, and we proceeded on our way to Norwich.

As it turned out, my Dad completely misunderstood my Mom's intentions and assumed we would all be waiting for him back in Noank that evening. For our part, we could see the boat looked undamaged and appeared to be floating about on her waterline. What we couldn't see, and the communication failure prevented us from knowing, was there were several holes in her bottom and my Dad had just spent 3 hours pumping her out. He attempted to start the engine, but the wiring was completely soaked. In addition, there was salt water in the crank-case and he could not get either the magneto or the distributor to produce a spark. Resigning himself to the unpleasant fact that he would have to leave the badly leaking boat where it was, he did his best to plug the worst leaks with rags. Then, having done all he could to save her, he borrowed a large rowboat from a Mr. Lee, who owned the dock, and loaded it with as much gear from the *ANNA R* as it would safely carry without swamping.

He didn't get underway until after sundown and the trip home was, as he put it in his diary, a hard pull. He told me about it later and it was all that and then some. It was only about a mile and a half trip from Mr. Lee's dock to our home, but the big rowboat was loaded to the gunnels and was a brute to handle. There was also a strong SW breeze right on the nose and, before he rounded Sixpenny Island, it was pitch dark. The skies had been overcast to begin with and, with all of the wires down from the storm, there wasn't a light to be seen anywhere along the coast. He told me he rowed and rowed, until it didn't seem as if he could pull another stroke. When you stop and think about it, it had to have been an exhausting experience for him. In addition to the stress of the preceding day and little sleep that night, he had walked the railroad tracks from Noank to Mystic and from there to Masons Island in his hip boots, pumped steadily for three hours to float the boat and hadn't had as much as a drink of water since breakfast. There wasn't even any sky-glow to give him the silhouette of the beach and, although he knew he ought to be about abreast of our house, he was physically and emotionally drained from the ordeal and really had no clear idea of his exact location.

He stopped rowing for a moment to catch his breath and to see if there was some way he could determine his position relative to the land. He finally saw a dim light sweeping around on the shore and he called out that he needed someone to guide him to where our dock used to be. A shout came back immediately "Is that you out there Benny?" My Dad answered "It sure is, shine the light on the rocks so I can see enough to land safely." In a few minutes, Halstead Brown, Ivan Crossman and Dr. Roland Hill, who had been looking for him after he failed to show up at Halstead's by dark, helped him stagger up the beach. Dr. Hill sat him down on a rock, took his pulse and checked him over, while the other two unloaded the skiff and lugged the gear up to the house. Dr. Hill then gave my Dad strict orders to have a hot meal, go straight to bed and get some badly needed rest.

In the morning, my Mother and Aunt Katherine left us two kids in Norwich in charge of my grandfather and drove back down to Noank. On the way, they swung by Willow Point, just in case my Dad had spent the night aboard the boat. They had the unpleasant task of telling him there was no need to hurry back up

ANNA R I *hauled out at Wildes' Boatyard (now Ford's Lobsters) after the 1938 hurricane. Dad (left) and Elmer Davis (right). Rossie mill (now University of Connecticut Marine Lab) in background.*

ANNA R I *ready for launching, spring 1939.*

to pump it out, because the *ANNA R* had sunk during the night and only the foredeck and the pilothouse were showing at high water. Although the bad news was a big set back, there was other work which also had to be done. As soon as my Aunt left to return to her supervisors job at the Carpenter Manufacturing Co in Norwich, my Mom and Dad began the job of boarding up the broken front windows and mopping out the inside of the house to make it at least partly liveable. Nevertheless, by midday my Dad couldn't stand thinking about the boat lying there submerged and he rowed up after lunch to see if he could do anything to raise her. There really wasn't, but while he was there he ran a line from the mast over to the dock to keep her from falling over when the tide went down and dove down into the flooded cabin to salvage the rest of the fishing gear. Satisfied that he had done all he could without additional manpower, he loaded up the skiff again and brought the soggy mess home in case we had another bad storm and the *ANNA R* broke up before he was able to figure out how raise her.

Two days later, my Aunt Katherine brought my brother and me back down to Noank so we could return to school. We arrived just in time to see the *ANNA R* being towed down the river by William and Ashby Anderson in the Anderson family's boat *BINGO*, which had been tied up at Franklin Post's dock in Mystic and was one of the few boats that escaped the hurricane unscathed. The railroad swing bridge over the Mystic River was still inoperative, so Will and Ashby wrestled the mast out of *BINGO* and managed to squeeze under the bridge at low water. The raising of the *ANNA R* is a story in itself for the entire shoreline area was still under a state of emergency. Fortunately, one of Dad's best customers, Gladden Baker, was treasurer of the Travelers Insurance Company and had used his considerable influence to get a special pass from the Governor allowing him to travel anywhere in the state. Gladden also knew manpower alone would not be enough to raise a sunken boat. Armed with his very official looking pass, he walked right into the Connecticut State Guard warehouse and commandeered a couple of big hand pumps and some heavy duty tackles. He then picked up three other Traveler's executives, stopped by Noank for my Dad and, by dint of a desperate effort aided by a low tide, they had floated the *ANNA R.*

Although they had achieved their original objective, the old boat was leaking like a sieve and was only being kept afloat by the impromptu crew continually manning the State of Connecticut's hand pumps. Hauling her out at a boatyard was out of the question, for all the marine railways in this area were either completely wrecked or blocked by debris, giving them no choice but to run the *ANNA R* up on the beach where Ford's Lobsters is today. There she sat, rocking slowly to and fro while my Dad ran guy ropes from the masthead to keep her from falling over at low tide. He then bored a 3/4 inch hole through the oak stem at the waterline and ran a short piece of chain through it to make a strap. Meanwhile, his helpers wrestled several heavy planks under the keel to make a skid for the steel rollers my Mom was hacksawing out of some junk pipe we had dragged from the wreckage. It was late afternoon before all preparations were completed but, before Dad's volunteer helpers had to start back to Hartford, the heaviest tackle was attached to a crowbar driven deeply into the ground, and an attempt was made to haul the *ANNA R* up the bank. It was a good try but turned out to be a dismal failure. The tide was rising and the boat was bouncing around a bit as she lifted. This loosened the planks under the keel, allowing them to spread apart a bit, which then let the rollers fall off the planks and jam under the keel. This happened several times and my Dad was finally forced to abandon the effort for the time being.

All told, it took about a week of intermittent effort to get the boat hauled up far enough to be safe from high water. It all had to be done by hand and progress depended to a great extent on how many bodies were available to pull on the ropes. My Dad had some help the next day from Captain Francke and one or two others, but everyone in Noank had big troubles of their own to overcome and they could only stay until the boat was grounded solidly. The struggle to pull the boat up the beach went on intermittently for more than a week and most of the time there were only four of us from the family (two adults and two kids) laboring away at the task. When reduced to this number, we had to use the original double sheave main tackle, a double sheave luff tackle and a single whip tackle for a luff on the luff. As you can readily imagine, progress under those conditions was measured in inches not feet. Eventually, the original volunteer gang returned bringing reinforcements and, with their added muscle power, we got the old girl high enough to be out of the reach of any normal storm tide and put the *ANNA R* to bed until spring.

The rest of the fall my brother John and I spent every daylight moment after school helping our parents. We climbed up on the steeply sloping roof to help pull nails and handed up lumber while the adults boarded up holes in the walls. However, our primary chore was to drag wreckage out of the piles of debris and begin cutting firewood for the coming winter, as it was a sure bet we wouldn't have much money to spare for coal or kerosene. I guess you could say we went through some pretty hard times during the next several years, but we never went hungry or without proper clothing and we were kept so busy between school and our jobs helping heat and rebuild the house that we never had time to feel we were disadvantaged by our circumstances.

1938 Hurricane aftermath. Edna Jones'house (now John Rathbun's) on left, our house in background. Wrecked automobile belonged to Hadley Fitch.

Chapter Seven

SOME ELDRIDGE
BOATSHOP TALES

(Mostly told to me by my Dad)

Noank had long been highly regarded for the sturdy fishing boats which local craftsmen built in the various yards along her shores but, by the time I came along, the only boat-builder still in business was Webster (Webb) Eldridge. Before the 1938 hurricane there were actually two Eldridge yards, a main yard at the foot of Spring Street, where Bob Whittaker's boatyard is today, and a satellite yard at the site of the present Golden Era Boats in Spicer's Noank Marina. Before it was destroyed in the 1938 hurricane, the yard on Spring Street was where almost all the new boats were constructed, with the facility on the west side of the cove mainly used for small boat repair and general storage. I was only 10 years old at the time of the hurricane, so my memories of the main boatyard on Spring Street are a jumbled hodgepodge of events I actually witnessed and stories related to me by my Dad. Which ones are which is really not very important, but I want to clarify at the outset that I was not physically present at all the events I am going to describe.

I was too young to have known "Webb" Eldridge personally, but from all accounts his temperament would have been best described as mercurial. However correct that judgment may be, I do know that his unsolicited offer to build a new boat for my Dad, when we were literally down and out after the 38 hurricane, shows he was also generous to a fault. After all, not everyone would propose to build a boat for someone who had no down payment, next to no present income and a very questionable ability to pay for the boat in a timely manner. It was not my Dad's idea at all. According to what my Dad told me, Webb just decided my Dad needed to replace the leaky old converted catboat he had bought from Otto Hendrickson in 1930; end of subject.

As I mentioned in the preceding chapter, my Dad's boat named *ANNA R*, our family's name for all its fishing boats since 1924, had been seriously damaged in the 1938 hurricane when it pulled the headfast over the top of the stake and was

MADELYN launching. Left to right, Bob Whittaker, Howard Davis, Bill Lord, Fred Story, Ivan Crossman.

Hauling MADELYN out of the boatshop, Ivan Crossman in foreground. Note: the boat is facing west. Launched Spring 1948.

Ivan and Errol Crossman's FALCON nearing completion, September 1946.

Ivan Crossman making a command decision on FALCON.

ANNA R II *at Eldridge Boatyard, my Dad in foreground.*
Photographer: Al Haring.

driven against a rocky outcropping on Masons Island. Although it had been successfully salvaged and the holes in the bottom repaired during the winter, Webb had always maintained that proper repairs were never going to be possible, for the boat was more than 45 years old and had been structurally unsound even before the hurricane. I know from reading my Dad's 1939 diaries that he had to haul the *ANNA R* out of the water three or four times during the summer, in what turned out to be a series of vain attempts to bring the leaks under control. Bob Whittaker and Ivan Crossman would pound in more boat nails and recaulk the leaking seams as best they could, and it would be OK for awhile. Unfortunately, the next rough day she would resume leaking like a proverbial sieve and Dad would have to haul the old girl out again to keep her from sinking overnight.

During one of the last of these frustrating episodes, Webb came out of the shop and buttonholed my Dad. "Benny" he said, "that old boat is going to drown you some rough day. We just can't keep her planking from loosening up again because most of the ribs and butt blocks are about shot and they simply won't hold nails any more. I'll tell you what I've decided to do. I haven't got enough work to keep my people busy all winter, so I'm going to build you a new boat to keep from laying them off. I've salvaged a few molds from the wreckage of the other shop and I can just eyeball the rest of the shape. I figure in order to do both commercial fishing and carry your fishing parties, she ought to be about 31 feet long and be a combination of my lobsterboat model and the charterboat I built for Max Langworthy. Furthermore, if you can take the engine out of the old boat by yourself, it will help to keep the cost down even more."

My Dad was really stunned at this offer and just stood there for a couple of minutes. He finally found his voice and replied "Webb, how in the world am I going to pay for this boat, I can barely make enough money to feed my family and heat the house, let alone pay you for a new boat?" "Benny", Webb replied, "I wasn't asking you if you wanted to have me build a boat, I was telling you that I'm going to do it. I figure that, with this new boat, you will be able to make enough extra money to pay me off in a couple of years and have cash to spare. I've got to keep my men busy and I know that you need a new boat if you're going to stay fishing, so it's all settled. Here, we'll shake on it." With that he reached out, grabbed my Dad by the hand and gave it a shake. "There, it's done" he said and stalked back into the shop, leaving my Dad standing there dumfounded. Webb, as always, meant exactly what he said and in the spring of 1940 he launched a new 32 footer for us, at a total cost of only $2,500.00. In the meantime, my Dad had taken apart the old 30 horse 3-cylinder Lathrop, piece by piece, and reassembled it in the new boat where it performed yeoman duty for another ten years. As an indication that Webb's confidence was not unwarranted, my Dad's diary for Thursday, September 21, 1944 had the following entry. "Went over to Clara Eldridge's. (Webb's widow) Paid the last payment on *ANNA R*. She gave me a nice coat and a pair of rubbers. Boys got more railroad ties today. We now have 21 ties."

Another side to Webb's personality which differed markedly from his normal affability and generosity was his extremely short temper. As a matter of fact, explosive would be a good description of Webb's disposition, for he could go from congenial to enraged in the blink of an eye. One of my Dad's often related Eldridge Boatshop anecdotes, which illustrates this aspect, told of a day while the entire gang, Webb included, were planking a new boat and Webb accidentally bashed his thumb with his favorite hammer. He let out a string of expletives, stalked to the door that overlooked the water and threw the hammer as far out into West Cove as he could. "There, you blankety blank so and so, you'll never have the chance to do that to me again" he shouted after it. The next day he spent the entire morning in a skiff, jabbing around in the mud with an eel spear trying to retrieve his hammer.

Other explosions would often occur when they were bending the ribs for a hull under construction. The wood for the ribs was always cut from very carefully selected, knot free, oak stock before being placed in the steambox, but as any wooden boatbuilder can attest, every so often a frame will crack or split while it is being bent. The first time this took place, Webb would usually grumble a little but keep right on working; the second time would produce a moderate amount of cussing among the crew, but if it happened two times in a row, all Hell would break loose. First there would be a volcano of cuss words from Webb; then the following would usually take place. "Gimme that blankety blank frame." Webb would bellow at the others. Grabbing it out of their hands, he would stamp down to the big bandsaw at the east end of the shop and throw the offending stick of wood on the table. He would then step over to the ancient 4-cylinder Chevrolet engine that powered both the bandsaw and planer and try to start it. At this point everyone in the shop was hoping against hope that the old Chevvy would start readily, for if it didn't, it too might be in grave danger. After coaxing (and often kicking) the engine into reluctant life, Webb would slide the flat drive-belt over onto the saw pulley and let the saw come up to speed. Now, the length of time it took to do all this rigamarole would have been enough to calm most anybody down, but not Webb. The longer it took, the madder he became, especially if he didn't let the engine warm up enough and it sputtered to a stop when he put a load on the bandsaw. He would cut the offending stick of wood up into virtually bite-sized pieces, collect them in a basket and dump them into the woodstove. "There you blankety blank so and so," he'd growl. "You'll never split on me again." He would then turn around and go back to work as if nothing had ever happened.

Webb was also a dyed in the wool practical joker and would go to incredible lengths to plan and pull one off. Everyone who visited the shop had to be on guard every minute. You never laid anything down if you could avoid it and, if you did, you had better keep your eyes on it at all times. Sometimes Webb would wait for weeks for a particular person to arrive so that a carefully orchestrated plan could be put into play. If, for instance, you came in to have some lath cut and you made the mistake of leaving the bundle unwatched for a few moments, it would almost certainly be nailed to something or a long string would be attached that would jerk it out of your hands when you walked away. Boots were nailed to the floor, hats to their pegs, coat-sleeves sewed up and so on. He once even managed to nail a sleeping drunk's shoe to the floor by carefully toe-nailing the sole down. Webb then woke him up with the cry of "FIRE" and the boatshop crew all stampeded out the door. The poor man thought his leg had gone to sleep or had somehow become paralyzed and he was frantically slapping it around trying to get the circulation back while, at the same time, hollering frantically for help at the top of his lungs.

One of my Dad's favorite Eldridge Boatyard stories involved his close friend Ivan Crossman and, as best as I can recall, went like this. One winter day, Ivan borrowed the work skiff and Webb's eel-spear during his lunch hour and rowed out into West Cove to try his luck. To everyone's surprise he did quite well and came back with about a dozen big eels squirming around in the bottom of a nail keg. For those of you who are fairly young, nails did not always come in cardboard boxes, nor were they usually made in third-world countries. In those bygone days, they came packed in wooden kegs and both the nails and their containers were made in America. Anyway, it was time to go back to work, so the keg and its writhing contents were stored under one of the workbenches until quitting time. Now, skinning eels (called *dressing* for some obscure reason) is not something that everybody wants to learn to do, but Ivan liked his eels skinned and had a well deserved reputation as being very skillful at that arcane trade. Webb quizzed him several times about how long it was going to take to skin the

12 or 13 eels after they got through work. "I'd really like to watch you" he said "but I don't want to be late for dinner." "Ha" retorted Ivan, "I'll show you a thing or two about skinning eels and you won't be late for dinner by a damn-sight." "OK" said Webb, "but it better be quick as I'm not going to hang around all evening while you mess around with those slimy devils." There was no comment from Ivan.

Quitting time came and the demonstration was next in order. "You've got to have a very sharp knife," said our hero, as he carefully honed his favorite Dexter fillet knife. "Soon as I get a good edge on this blade, I'll show you how to get those little beauties out of their jackets in nothing flat." "After all this buildup, it had damn well better be fast," said Webb, making a big show of taking out his pocket watch to check the time. "Watch this," was the reply from our champion as he reached deep into the keg and grasped one of the eels by the head. Up it came, but only for a little way, as it slowly slipped through his fingers and slithered back down into the keg. "Damn" mumbled Ivan and made another grab. This time he used a careful grip and pulled slowly and steadily upwards, but the eel seemed too slippery to hold onto and down it slid, back with the others. "Well, what the hell are you waiting for, I haven't got all night," groused Webb. There was no comment from the obviously frustrated eel skinner, as he strode over to the woodstove, scooped some ashes from the pit, dumped then into the keg and shook it around to mix the ashes with the eels. "There, that'll take care of this little problem and you'll be able to get home for supper on time. Just be a little more patient for gosh sakes," said the somewhat flustered fisherman. But it was still no good for, ashes or not, the eels continued to slip through his hands and slide back down to join their fellow captives. By this time, Ivan finally realized he was the unwitting butt of another of Webb's pranks. He grabbed up the keg, turned it over and, sure enough, the eels were all hanging there head down, with their tails nailed securely to the bottom of the keg.

There were other incidents, such as the time they were getting ready to roll a just completed boat out the door. In new construction, it was common practice for Webb to secure the blocked-up keel to the floor of the shop by boring a hole down through the keel, the blocking and the wooden floor and fastening everything together using a long steel rod which had been threaded at both ends. This was to keep the hull from shifting in any direction and had the added benefit of preserving the previously calculated declivity from having to be reset. The shop was, and still is, built on piers with a low crawl space underneath and one of the workmen would be delegated to crawl under the building in order to unscrew the nut from the bottom of the bolt. Webb, being a keen student of human nature, knew just whom to send down to do the job. One of his men was always questioning him about every little detail and was obviously intensely curious. Webb figured, and rightly so as it turned out, that when this employee had removed the nut and the bolt had been withdrawn, he would squint up through the hole to see if it was all clear. However, as soon as the bolt was completely out of the keel, Webb had a cup of water ready and poured some down the hole, at the same time yelling "for God's sake guys, don't pee down the hole!" Sure enough, a tremendous roar came from under the building, followed by coughing, retching and the sound of a body thrashing around. Everybody in the shop was convulsed in laughter when the door burst open and the victim of the joke charged in shouting "Where is he? I'm gonna kill the son of a B**** that pissed down that hole." Webb was laughing so hard it was several minutes before he could regain his composure and explain that it was all a joke.

Another classic prank was pulled off at the expense of the local Sea Scout troop. They had been given a used surfboat, of which they were naturally very proud, and one fine summer day they made the mistake of sailing into Webb's dock and asked him if they could leave the boat tied up there unattended for awhile. Webb said it wouldn't be a problem and the young men trudged happily off on their errand. As soon as they were out of sight, Webb had the yard crew haul the boat far enough up the rowboat ramp for him to bore a hole through the keel near the bow, to which he fastened about 10 fathoms of old potwarp. When this was accomplished, they quickly launched the boat and returned it to its place at the dock. Webb next tied a rock weighing about 50 pounds to the end of the rope, dropped it into a work skiff and rowed it out as far into West Cove as the length of the line permitted.

They finished just in time, for the boys soon returned in full uniform, along with their leader. You could see right away that the departure was going to conform to proper ritual for the quartermaster piped the captain aboard and all orders were given in the correct naval form. The breeze was blowing at right angles to the dock so, after unfurling the mainsail and getting ready to hoist the jib, they prepared to sail away from the wharf. The coxswain stood braced on the aft deck, grasped the tiller firmly in his right hand and gave orders in a clear voice. "All hands, prepare to get underway, drop the centerboard, up mainsail and jib." When everybody was in the proper position, he gave the command to cast off and away they went.

It was a stirring sight. The old surfboat gathered way smartly in the gentle breeze and had gone about 100 feet when it suddenly skidded to a stop. The leader picked himself up off the deck and looked around to see if anybody was watching them. There was nobody in sight but, unbeknown to them, all of Webb's crew were peeking out at them through the boatshop's grimy windows. The Scouts naturally felt they had hit something on the bottom with the centerboard and there was a flurry of orders to haul it up. That done, they made ready to take off again but, in the meantime, the boat had drifted down-wind until it had almost fetched up on the line attached to the rock.

The sails were quickly sheeted in again and they set off close-hauled on the port tack. As soon as the boat began to gather steerage way, it was plain to everyone aboard that something was radically wrong. They didn't know what was causing the problem, but the boat was absolutely determined to come up into the wind no matter how hard over the coxswain pulled the tiller. It slewed sharply to port and instead of hesitating there in stays for a moment, snapped right around on the other tack. The jib now was aback and you would have expected the boat to bear off sharply, but no such luck; it went only a few feet and came up short again, right into the wind. Things aboard were in an uproar, with the skipper calling out orders left and right and total confusion reigning in the ranks. About then, somebody aboard the boat finally looked ashore and noticed Webb rolling around on the ground, laughing fit to kill, and the light slowly dawned on them that they too had been had.

Another variation of this caper was played on an elderly gentleman who rowed across the cove in a flat bottomed skiff almost every winter day for a visit. He would normally hang around the shop for at least several hours, chatting with the workers or whoever else happened to drop by. Before leaving to row back home, he always scrounged up every piece of scrap lumber he could lay his hands on to use for his own stove. This practice began to annoy Webb a bit, for he also depended on scrap wood to heat the boatshop and he decided to send the old gent a message in the form of a practical joke. It went like this. One day when Webb knew the tide was falling, he had some of the crew sneak out and quietly haul the victim's skiff up the small boat ramp which used to lie on the north side of the dock. They then rolled the skiff up on its side and nailed a fairly large wooden box to the bottom. During this clandestine activity, Webb made sure the big surface planer was running to mask any noise coming from outside while he kept his victim occupied inside the shop by helping him gather up an unusually large amount of firewood to take home. After several hours had gone by, Webb figured the tide had fallen enough for his scheme to succeed and he feigned one of his infamous temper tantrums. As expected, the unsuspecting visitor quickly excused himself and made ready to row home. It was fairly deep alongside the dock and, although the heavily loaded skiff seemed to move very sluggishly, the old timer dug in his oars and began to make slow headway across the cove. He got about a third of the way across before the box grounded in the mud and there he stopped. First, he stuck down an oar to check the depth. Finding it nearly three feet deep he next peered over the side to see if he was hung-up on a mooring. Again, no dice. He then began to prod around under the boat with an oar and in a few minutes found he, too, had been made the butt of one of Webb's practical jokes.

The last boatshop tale I am going to relate was an unplanned affair which took place while the yard had a lobsterboat hauled out on the marine railway for hull and engine repairs. Webb was working under the boat on the keel while the mechanic, I believe it was Raymond Ledwood, and the owner were in the cabin rebuilding the carburetor. Back in those days, the rubber impeller, Jabsco type seawater coolant pump had not come on the scene and many of the marine engines used a mechanical piston pump which could run dry for a long time before becoming damaged. Because there was no complicated water connection necessary, it was not at all unusual for a mechanic to run an engine while the boat was on the railway or stored in the boatyard. The only precaution was to notify anybody working outside to keep well clear of the propeller. The boat they were working on that particular day was one of Webb's standard 28 footers, all of which had only crouching headroom in the cabin that also doubled as an engine compartment. The engine in question was one of the 20 HP 2-cylinder hand-start

Lathrops, so naturally there was the usual priming routine going on before-hand, with a lot of huffing and puffing coming from both the engine and the operators as they rolled the big flywheel over with the starting bar. "Stay clear, Webb," shouted the mechanic as he got ready to give a mighty heave that would, hopefully, start the motor on the first try.

Webb heard the mechanic give a loud grunt as he flung the flywheel over with all his might. Quick as a wink, Webb reached down, grabbed an 8 foot long 1X3 inch slat that was lying on the ground and struck the bottom of the boat under the turn of the bilge as hard as he could. The flat board made a surprisingly loud boom, followed in quick succession by a muffled thunk coming from the cabin of the boat. Then nothing for another few seconds. All of a sudden, out of the cabin staggered the mechanic with blood streaming down his face from a cut on top of his head. The board had made such a loud noise in the cabin that he instinctively thought the engine had exploded. Naturally, he involuntarily straightened up, banged his head on the oak deck beams and cut his scalp to the bone on a bolt sticking down through the beam. He was mad as Hell, but Webb thought it was a huge joke and it couldn't have gone over better if he had planned it for a week.

My Dad's boat was launched in the spring of 1940. Webb's eyeball design using salvaged molds from previously built boats proved to be very successful and attracted considerable interest along the waterfront. Mr. Robert Newell, a summer resident of Groton Long Point, came over to look at the *ANNA R* on several occasions. I guess he liked what he saw, for he placed an order with Webb to build a boat of the same hull design, but with a more yacht-like interior. Mr. Newell's *CELESTIA* was launched in the spring of 1941. She turned out to be Webb's final boat because the outbreak of World War II put a virtual halt to boat building activities at the Eldridge yard, except Webb kept a skeleton crew busy with storage and repair work.

When Webb died suddenly in 1944, his widow, Clara, continued to operate the yard until Bob Whittaker returned from his wartime job at Electric Boat. With Bob in charge, new construction soon followed as Ivan and Errol Crossman's *FALCON* took shape. The *FALCON* was also built on the same molds as the *ANNA R* and the *CELESTIA*, but the decks and superstructure were those of a conventional lobsterboat. Other boats, both sail and power, quickly followed. Among them were Jack Wilbur's *STAR* (a slightly enlarged and modified *ANNA R* design) and the Chapman brothers' lobsterboat *WALLACE B* (another modified *ANNA R* hull). A tribute to Webb Eldridge and his *protégé* successor Bob Whittaker is that these boats built from Webb's cobbled up *ANNA R* model are still around, although not all in the best of condition. The 56 year old *ANNA R* was in almost daily use until 2 years ago and is tied behind the New London Sewage plant; *CELESTIA* has been restored at great expense and is still yachting in Buzzards Bay; the *FALCON* is hauled out in Niantic and being refurbished by her new owner Paul Bates; the *STAR* is in constant use by Mystic Seaport, but the *WALLACE B* is rotting away in Baker's Cove.

While Mary Anderson and I were going over the pictures for this story, she noticed that, in one picture, the *ANNA R* had her bow facing toward the

ANNA R II after being hauled out of boatshop. Note: the boat is facing east, 1940.

ANNA R II on launching cradle, now facing west.

ANNA R II Launch day. Left to right, Webster Eldridge, Dad, Ivan Crossman, Bob Whittaker.

boathouse, and in another picture, her stern was facing the boathouse. This reminded me that Webb always built his boats with the bow pointed in an easterly direction. Just about all boats are launched stern first and, when his shop was on the east shore of the cove, it was entirely proper to build them facing east. Whether from stubbornness, or more likely superstition, Webb continued this practice when he moved his base of operation to the west shore of the cove after the 1938 hurricane. There, building the boats with the bow pointed eastward meant that, after the boats were hauled stern-first out of the boatshop, they had to be turned 180 degrees before they could be placed on the launching cradle. Needless to say, turning a 30 foot boat around on the sloping ground was not an easy task, but Webb refused to do it any other way. When Bob Whittaker took over the operation of the yard after Webb passed away, he threw tradition aside and built the *FALCON* with her bow facing west, and you know what? She didn't sink, so the rest of Bob's boats, including the one he and I built together in 1958-1959, were built facing west.

While I don't believe it is unlucky to build a boat with its bow facing west, I would never again allow a boat of mine to be launched on a Friday. Most people are unaware that launching on Friday, whistling while underway, turning a hatch cover upside down, using blue paint on your boat and having yellow oilskins on board are old Yankee superstitions which most of today's enlightened boaters consider to be foolish. I used to feel the same way, and during the many years I spent on the water, I violated all of them. It would be nice to say there were no ill effects from this flagrant flaunting of tradition and, except for launching on Friday, this is correct. Three times I launched on a Friday and each time I had potentially disastrous accidents when underway.

ANNA R II Underway on launch day. John, me and "Pal". Dad at helm, 1940.

The first time I launched on a Friday, I soon became a member of what is known locally as "The Horseshoe Reef Club." I accomplished this feat one foggy night, back in the days before radar and loran, by running over the rocks on Horseshoe Reef at 8 knots and nearly wrecking my new boat. The second time I violated the Friday rule I nearly ran between a tug and a huge steel barge one foggy morning. The tug wasn't blowing his foghorn and the first inkling I had that we were steaming into danger was seeing the towline looming through the fog right in front of my boat. I spun the wheel hard over but we were so close we hit the towline with the side of the boat. Fortunately the towline didn't foul our propeller and we missed the oncoming barge by about 10 feet.

Any reasonable person would have "Got the Message" after that scare, but I dismissed the connection as just another Old Wives' Tale and gave it no credence. Almost 10 years passed before I again defied tradition and deliberately launched on a Friday. It took a few months before the hex, or whatever you wish to call it, struck back at the unbeliever. This time the autopilot refused to disengage after I dialed-in a 10 degree course change to miss a lobsterpot buoy and kept right on turning the boat to starboard. I tried desperately to stop it by shutting the unit off, but it was too late. While jabbing futilely at the buttons (I had taken my eyes off the "Road," as it were) and before I could slow the boat down from her 10 knot cruising speed, we nailed Silver Eel bell buoy dead center and knocked a hole in the bow about 6 inches above the waterline. You don't have to be Sherlock Holmes to know I have absolutely no intention of EVER launching any boat of mine on a Friday. Scoff if you want, I don't care. It's "Three strikes and you're Out" for me, when it comes to my launching on Friday superstition.

Although change is inevitable, these boats from Webb Eldridge and Bob Whittaker signify the end of an era. We didn't know it at the time, but Webb's *ANNA R* model was the final chapter in the evolution of Noank lobster boats from the catboats and well smacks of the 18th and 19th centuries. Even though a few wooden pleasure craft are still being built and repaired locally, Webb and Bob's masterful products will almost certainly be the last wooden "work" boats of their size to be built in Noank. As such, they represent the end of Noank's wooden commercial shipbuilding tradition, which began in the early 1700s, saw its perigee in the Palmer Shipyard of the late 1800s and essentially ended with the 40 foot wooden charterboat Bob Whittaker and I launched in the spring of 1959.

Chapter Eight

The Hurricane of September 14, 1944

Copied verbatim from a report written by B. F. Rathbun Sr.
(The words enclosed in parenthesis are mine)

On the afternoon of Sept. 13th I heard at the Electric Boat Company, where I was employed, that a hurricane was due to strike at 4 P.M. The men were securing the subs and things around the docks. I was sure from the looks of the weather that there was no immediate danger from a storm so I remained until the whistle blew. Upon my reaching home Anna told me that the radio was reporting a hurricane coming up the coast due to hit the Carolinas some time during the night. The storm itself was traveling at about 15 miles per hour with high winds. The barometer was steady and no wind so I left the *ANNA R* at the stake for the night. All through the evening the radio gave warnings of the storm. We retired for the night and set the alarm clock for 5:15, my usual rising time. When I arose I turned on the radio and after Anna got up we got the report that the storm's rate of travel had increased to 18 miles and that it was due to hit the Connecticut-Rhode Island line at midnight. I did not go to work but went about the house fixing the blinds so they would close. I brought the *ANNA R* into the dock where I could get going at short notice. Meanwhile the reports from the Carolinas told of severe damage in the storm's wake.

When B.F. and J.A. (myself and my brother John) came home (from school) we finished securing things around the house, nailed up the front and back door, nailed boards over some of the front windows and roofing paper over the others. I had made a cradle to use hauling B.F.'s sailboat. Anna made arrangements to store the boat at Haring's. After fixing the house we hauled the sailboat at Haring's with the help of several bystanders. I then went to Mystic in the *ANNA R*, taking "Wes" Morrill with me for the ride. By this time the wind was freshening from the South. Anna had called up Lathrop's and they told her I could tie up at their wharf. There were several large fishing boats from Stonington there and I

ANNA R II *at dock on Riverview Avenue, about 1941.*

kept moving my boat so I could be on the outside as I was afraid to be between such large boats. Bill Musante's old boat *FRANCIS* came up and I finally tied up outside her. I ran my lines over onto the dock itself and had lines on her stern and bit forward, as well as a spring line. Boats coming from everywhere seeking places of safety as the report said the storm would hit us about 9 P.M. with a 9 ft. tide rise and 70-80 mile gales.

Just before dark I called Anna and told her I was coming home. I had not eaten since morning. It was blowing hard from the NE and raining very hard. I took the bus to Noank and when I came through the road by Langworthy's I hit the wind. It was really something and I knew from the other hurricane that we were in for a severe time. We ate dinner and I found that the Crossmans had extended an invitation to our family to spend the night with them. As I did not know how much water would come in as the result of the storm I advised the family to go to the Crossman's for the night. Anna and John went over to our neighbors the Davis' and told them we were leaving so Mel decided to go to New London to his mother's for the night. He took Anna up to Crossmans in his car. While Anna and John were going over to Mel's, our flag pole crashed (down) just missing Anna. I went up and took the bus for Mystic as I had decided to remain with the boat for the night. After I got on the bus it rained so hard the driver could see only with the greatest difficulty. In front of Securo's a wire was across the road arcing so we had to back up and go over Prospect Hill and down Collins' Hill, thence to Mystic. It was 8:00 P.M. and dark.

I got down aboard the boat and decided to put out more lines. I got them ready and then found I was unable to pull the *FRANCIS* in to jump on the dock. Things were so wild by now that I had no desire to remain on the boat but, not being able to get on to the dock, I had no choice in the matter. I then took my new anchor cable and tied it to the bitt and led the rope back into the cockpit and made the anchor ready to throw over at a moments notice. No one appeared to take care of the *FRANCIS* but Bert Ford (on the *CATHERINE)* and some fishermen from Stonington on the *MATOSA* were around on their boats. They finally went below and I did the same. I started the engine to warm it up in case I had to leave the dock. The wind was really blowing now and the rain (was) beating down. I let the engine run and sat looking out the lee port light to be sure we did not get loose and blow down on the boats below me. The wind was still NE. It blew in gusts of short duration, then (there) would be a short lull, then a terrific blast would hit us. I watched the barometer drop, drop and I reset the gold hand every now and then. Finally it reached 28.45 where it stopped. The time was about 11 P.M. I soon noticed the wind had dropped and the stars were shining brightly. I went out and looked around. I put on my searchlight and saw that the spiles on the dock were under water and that water seemed to be up to the houses across the river.

The tide was ebb but sticks, etc. were coming "up" the river very rapidly. The *MATOSA* had her deck lights on and there were men on deck. I knew that soon the wind would come from another quarter and we would go through the other side of the storm cycle. I thought it would be from the SW. I realized that unless the water fell very rapidly there was danger of being blown onto the dock, a prospect I did not relish. It was somewhere from 20-30 min. that the lull lasted. Not a breath of wind stirring, then suddenly from the NW came a gust and the rain again. I looked at the spiles and thought I could detect a slight fall in water. The wind now fairly screeched (and) the boats were pushed over against the dock. Bert Ford had men trying to keep his boat from going over the spiles. I found out after the storm that the big pole they use to hoist engines was keeping the boat from going over the spiles.

On our part (of the dock) there was nothing but low spiles and I would put my boat into reverse when the blasts came to keep my boat and the *FRANCIS* from going onto the dock. About this time I would have been very much satisfied to be on dry land. I fully expected to have to go out into the river and try to anchor and ride it out, but I decided to wait until the *FRANCIS* went on to the dock before I left. So I sat on the bow in the pouring rain and hung on to the bowstay to keep from being blown off the boat. I had a sharp knife in my hand and was waiting for the time to come when I would have to cut myself clear of the *FRANCIS*. I finally untied all the bow lines but one, this I could not untie, leaving my stern lines, 3 of them & a spring line. All the strain forward came upon the spring line as the wind was hitting my quarter and shoving me against the *FRANCIS* and ahead on the spring line. Things were rapidly getting worse but the tide had now fallen enough so that about 3 inches of the spiles were above water. About this time an extra severe gust came and I cut the bow line clear, leaped into the cockpit and reversed the engine. We did not go over the dock so for the next half hour I stood there in the pelting rain and wind reversing as I thought the need called for it.

When I could be sure that we would not be blown on top of the spiles I put the bow lines back on the boat once more. Now if my one spring line would keep me from shooting down upon the boats ahead, I knew I should come through with no damage to the boat. I let the engine run a while longer and sat in the cabin keeping my eyes on the boats ahead. After a while I went out and found that the dock itself was out of water. Bert Ford came along and asked if I was OK and we agreed that things were under control now. They retired to their boat and I went (down) into the cabin and lay down with my rain suit and southwester on listening to the wind which seemed to vary from W-NW but remained mostly in the NW. After a while it came from the W only and I knew I could try and get some rest. It was about 2:30 now so I took off my rain suit and layed on the locker. I was nearly exhausted and so tired I could not relax. The rain had stopped and I finally got some sleep. I awoke soon after daylight and as everything was OK and no one about I remained on the locker until 6:30, then I got up, went outside and started my Primus Stove and got some breakfast.

I took the 7:25 bus to Noank to find out how things were there. I met the boys at the bus and they told me they went down to the shore about 1 AM and with the help of Halstead Brown, Raymond Coon and Elbert Palmer got a line on my dock which had started to drift off. A piece of roofing paper had blown off the roof & our living room was a mess. The boys and I took the rug, pad, chair, etc. out in the yard to dry. B.F. and I then repaired the holes in the roof and started to take our deck off the dock. We worked until dark. Our lights came on about 6 PM but no telephone. The roof of the State Hatchery blew off and tore a section of Haring's roof off letting the rain into their house. B.F.'s sailboat received some minor scratches and cracked a plank or two. Art DeBiasi's boat sank at the stake and broke its mast. The *JEF* (Anderson's boat) sank at the dock. Mr.Newell's boat (the *CELESTIA*) got adrift and took the mooring with her but sustained no serious damage. The water was up to the top of our lower yard, but did not get into the cellar. Saturday we worked on the dock and all day Sunday and by the end of the day we had saved all that could be saved and things looked better. They raised the *JEF* and found her stern had been torn off. They patched her up and took her to Butson's (now Spicers' Noank Marina) to be hauled out. The storm was plenty severe for us but not like the one in 1938. Cape Cod suffered the most (damage) of all in New England.

Chapter Nine

BACK THEN WE THOUGHT IT WAS A PAIN IN THE NECK

NOW WE CALL THEM "THE GOOD OLD DAYS"

If you haven't actually lived through it, it is unlikely that you can have a true appreciation for the differences between fishing in the 1990s and fishing in the 1930s and 1940s. Now please don't get the impression I am yearning for the old way of life on the Sound, far from it. Except for the tremendous increase in traf-

Typical 1930s Noank fishing boats (rigged for dragging) at Noank Town Dock. Photo: Moses W. Rathbun Collection, Noank Historical Society, Inc.

fic, making a living as a so-called Waterman is certainly a lot less traumatic today than it was when I first began "messing around in boats." This fact is especially true during bad weather.

The changes encompass nearly all aspects of small-boat commercial fishing and include not only boats and equipment, but the attitudes of the fishermen as well. The local lobsterboats, having evolved from the Noank sloops and well-smacks of the late 1800s, were primarily 28 to 31 feet in length and were slack bilged (as opposed to a hard bilged "downeast" type), full displacement hulls having a top speed of 7 to 8 knots and, like all such hull forms, would be described by nautical "experts" as sea-kindly boats. However, when stripped of the stabilizing influence of their heavy masts and gaff rigged sails, they were really the wrong length and shape for the short, steep seas normally found in Long Island Sound. This caused them to jump around a lot in a head sea and roll heavily in a beam sea. I spent the first 16 years of my working life on one and, while they were certainly adequate at the time, the modern downeast type fiberglass boats now used by most full-time lobstermen do almost everything better and are much faster.

While boats are still boats, no matter how they are shaped or what they are made from, the tremendous advances in engines, fishing gear and electronics could never have been foretold by anyone. When I first started out in 1942, most of the fishermen were still in what I call the Joshua Slocum age of navigation and got by with a leadline, a compass and an alarm clock. While this may sound really romantic and be a source of pride to a yachtsman, I know from bitter experience that running in the fog and dark without electronics, when one has to do it day after day, erodes your nerves to the breaking point and makes you old before your time. Fog alone was bad; fog and dark was worse; fog, pitch dark and rough was harrowing and, if you add blowing snow to all that mess, a single mistake could cost you your life.

My Dad was an excellent boatman, but many days when we had chugged back from Montauk en route to Wicopisset passage at our normal cruising speed of 7 knots, we had to use what he called "AHAH" navigation, which usually went something like this. To begin with, my Dad always shaded our course slightly to the west, so if we had misjudged the set of the current we would meet up with Fishers Island instead of blundering onto the string of reefs which stretch from Fishers Island to Watch Hill. When we had about 5 minutes left before our ETA (estimated time of arrival) at Wicopisset bell bouy, we would shut down the engine and listen carefully while one of us took a sounding with one of the fishlines. If we could hear the bouy ding-donging away, everything was OK; if not, our next move was to idle in, taking a sounding every few minutes, until the surf could be heard. It was now Show Time and, with yours truly perched precariously on the bow, clinging grimly to the wire headstay and probably only half recovered from my normal foggy day bouts with seasickness, we would slowly nose the old girl in until I could make out the beach. If we had been commercial fishing and were alone on the boat, this was obviously a tense situation, but nothing we hadn't put up with many times before. However, if we had a fishing party aboard, many of our customers would now be in the process of graduating from worry to panic and be desperately in need of some assurance that we actually knew what we were doing, and that they were not doomed to have the phrase "Lost at Sea" engraved on their tombstones and never see their loved ones again.

"Blessed Assurance" was not long in coming for, as soon as the lookout shouted "LAND AHEAD" the engine would be reversed and the boat swung around while my Dad peered intently at the dim outline of the rocky shore. "AHAH" he would declare with great conviction and off we would chug parallel to the shore. He would then motion for me to come aft to the helm and would quietly mutter to me "Did you see anything you recognize?" The answer was, more likely than not, "Nope, how about you?" Without batting an eye or changing the expression of serene confidence he always adopted in those instances, he'd usually grunt "Me neither." This whole production would sometimes have to be repeated several times before one of us was able to recognize some feature on the shore or hear the bell-bouy that marked Wicopisset Passage. It should come as no surprise, that as soon as they became available after the war, we replaced the fishline method with a Raytheon depthsounder.

After the depthsounder, our next purchase was a marine radio and in contrast to the multitude of brands available today, immediately after the end of the war there were only a couple to choose between. The most commonly used set was the RCA, thousands of which had been placed aboard the offshore fishing boats during the war to assist in the submarine-watch program. The other contender was made by a little upstart firm called Ray Jefferson which was building some of the first high quality marine radios designed to be sold at a moderate price. The Ray Jeffersons were giving General David Sarnoff's RCA Corp. its first real taste of competition, so my Dad, who always rooted for the underdog, naturally bought a Ray Jefferson for our first set.

Before the marine radio became a common item on almost every boat, a fisherman who wanted to communicate boat to boat had only a couple of options. He could either get close enough to shout across the water or he could employ one or more of the hand and arm signals that had developed over the years. Often small groups of fishermen would modify these generic signals into a type of private code that was very much like the Signs that baseball coaches flash to their players. The audible option, called yelling or hollering around these parts, was effective over surprisingly long distances as long as the winds were light and the engines were shut off. I distinctly remember several occasions when Block Island handliners carried on lengthy "conversations" while anchored over a half mile apart. However, the use of the human voice to communicate a considerable distance can often lead to misunderstanding and confusion, as the following episode will plainly show.

In the years right after WW-I, the average Noank lobsterboat was often a recently converted catboat powered by a 2-cylinder, 16 HP make-and-break gas engine which could barely push the boat at 6 knots. At those speeds, it was necessary for a lobsterman, who wanted to haul two tides in the deep portion of the Race, to anchor close to the grounds between slack water periods because the

Typical Noank lobsterboats, 1920s-1930s.

swift current streaming through the Race at up to 6 knots causes the lobster buoys to be sucked underwater for all but about an hour on each side of slack water. Under fair weather conditions, most of the fishermen preferred to anchor abreast of the Race Point gun bunker at Fort Horatio G. Wright on Fishers Island, for there they could either rest or fish for blackfish. (Today, with 300 to 900 HP and 20+ knot lobsterboats, almost every Race lobsterman runs home to take out the catch between slacks.)

One of the local skippers, who always spent every minute of his spare time fishing, was a crusty old Norwegian-American World War I veteran named Ernst Francke. Now, Capt. Francke's personality was somewhat of a contradiction, for although he was a real loner, he had an almost insatiable curiosity and always did his utmost to find out what everyone else was doing. He was, however, particularly single-minded in his pursuit of the elusive blackfish, and it was common knowledge throughout the fleet that nothing could distract him from this endeavor.

The year in which the following episode took place, my Dad and his lifelong friend Ivan Crossman had teamed up in hopes of fame and fortune from lobstering and handlining blackfish. On that fateful day, they were anchored on the Nibbler ground north of Race Rock lighthouse about a quarter mile from Capt. Francke. It was a hot, flat calm day and, as is normal in those conditions, the fish were not biting very well. Most of the other locals had given up fishing altogether and were either sacked out or hollering back and forth. Not so for old Capt. Francke, he was hunched over, staring intently down into the water, tarred line wrapped tightly around his hand and poised to yank if a fish should be bold enough to bite.

My Dad always loved a practical joke and, more to relieve the boredom than anything else, he said to Ivan, "Whadda ya say we try ta get ol Captain Francke ta stop fishin." Ivan was very doubtful and countered, "He'd nevah do that no mattah what we did." My Dad took up the challenge, jumped to his feet, commenced to wave his arms around and started hollering a string of gibberish at the top of his lungs. "Conta-standa-feenish" he roared a couple of times while continuing to dance around and wave his arms. Lo and behold, Capt. Francke raised his head and hollered back, "Vot did you said?" Dad let go a second salvo of nonsense syllables and, wonder of wonders, Francke put down his handline, stood up and cupped his hand to his ear, "Vot did you said Benny?" he bellowed over the water. By this time the whole fleet had stopped fishing and was trying to figure out what the Sam Hill was going on. Encouraged by the success of his performance, Dad let fly another world-class conglomeration of sounds for his attentive audience. Francke didn't answer this time. He yanked in his handline, turned and went down into the cabin. "I guess he's mad at us and went down below ta have a cuppa coffee" Ivan said as both of them went back to fishing.

No sooner had they rebaited their hooks and let their lines down to bottom, than the unmistakable sound of a 2-cylinder Lathrop being started echoed across the water, chuff-chuff, pop-pop, pup-pup-pup it went. Every head in the fishing fleet swiveled around to see what was going on. The sounds were coming from Capt. Francke's boat and shortly he emerged from below, engaged the chain driven winch, put the boat in gear and began to haul the anchor. Dad and Ivan looked at each other in amazement. "Yuh don't suppose he's comin ovah heah?" said Ivan. "Naw, he's probably only movin ta a new spot ta get away from us," replied my Dad. But no, the lobsterboat, its grizzled old occupant standing at the wheel with his pipe clutched firmly in his teeth, was pointed straight at them. "Whot ya goin ta say ta him Ben?" "Don't know, Ivan." "Well, it bettah be good, cause he sure looks madder than a wet hen," Ivan retorted.

In a few minutes, the battered old craft was alongside them and Francke yelled over, "Vot in hell did you vant, Benny?" Dad stood there and with as straight a face as he could manage replied, "Ivan wants ta know if he kin jine the American Legion?" Francke almost exploded, "Vot iss da matta vith you Benny, you know he vasn't in da vor!" Dad just shrugged as if he had never even thought of that problem. Capt Francke's face began to turn a particularly deep shade of purple as he let loose with what were without doubt the strongest Norwegian cuss words at his command. He then slammed the engine into forward gear, yanked the throttle wide open, steamed back to where he was anchored before, threw the anchor overboard with a tremendous heave and went right back to fishing. Dad and Ivan, knowing full well they had barely escaped with a whole skin, took pains to avoid going near the old timer for the next two weeks, although they had to admit the result of the practical joke was certainly hilarious.

Nevertheless, if this incident didn't teach them a lesson, their next attempt at a theoretically harmless prank surely did. It took place in the same area and began when they noticed one of their anchored confederates had failed to appear on deck when it was time to get underway for the next slack. The missing lobsterman (I think it was Elmer Hewitt) had a habit of oversleeping and both of them naturally assumed he was down below snoring away. "Say Ivan, whadda ya say we wake him up by slidin alongside on our way by and tossin a rock inta the cockpit?" my Dad asked. "OK Benny, I'll just idle her down when we get close and you handle the rock," volunteered Ivan. Then, as now, beach stones in various sizes are used for supplemental pot ballast and all boats carry a few of them just in case they are needed. Dad grabbed a nice round one about the size of a large grapefruit and stood at the rail as Ivan slowly cruised by less than 10 feet from the anchored boat.

Dad made a smooth underhand toss, the rock curved gracefully through the air, landed with a resounding Whump on the port side deck, bounced into the air and disappeared from sight. There was a split second of silence and then a howl of pain from the cabin. In another moment the victim of their failed attempt at a joke came reeling out of the companionway clutching his head with his right hand and trying to hold the front of his pants away from his body with his left. "Just keep goin, Ivan," my Dad said. "We'll find out soon enough what happened. Right now, I think we'd better let him cool down some, cause he sure looks pretty upset, and he might try ta fire that rock through our pilothouse window if we go back alongside him again."

Later on they learned the wounded captain was not oversleeping, he was sitting on the locker eating a hot bowl of soup which he was holding on his lap. The rock had bounced on the rail, ricocheted through the companionway door, struck him a glancing blow on the head and dropped into the hot bowl of soup, which naturally smashed the bowl into a thousand pieces and filled his lap with hot chicken noodle soup. Fortunately for both the giver and the receiver, the unsolicited gift did no lasting damage, and all my Dad had to do to get off the hook was to buy a new bowl and a can of chicken soup. However, after this second practical joke backfired, both he and Ivan decided they had better quit before something went really wrong.

Chapter Ten

STEVE BAGNALL, NOANK SCHOONERMAN

It's strange how certain memories of your youth, which have been far from your thoughts during most of your adult life, begin to bubble up when you start to write about events only vaguely connected with them. They must be permanently tucked away in the remote recesses of your memory bank and only need to be triggered in some manner to rise up to the level of every-day consciousness. In my case, they don't come back as a whole series of total recollections, but emerge in small segments, as one thought seems to tease another out of hiding. For instance, I hadn't thought about Steve Bagnall for many years until I began putting a few of my memories about recess at Noank Grammar School on paper. Who, anyone under 50 will probably ask, was Steve Bagnall and why does he have a place in this hodgepodge of short stories? Well, although I only knew him at the end of his long life when he was merely the janitor at the school, he was one of the last of the fishermen who had worked aboard a Noank schooner at the turn of the century. This was during the period when internal combustion engines were first being installed in fishing vessels. Although there were several other schoonermen still living in Noank, such as Grover Eldredge, Charlie Hadley and Emil Coty, Steve was the only one I ever had the chance to actually sit down with and hear about some of the events which he experienced. Even as a youth, I was aware his stories should have been recorded but, like many of the things you mean to do, I never took the time to do it. As a consequence almost all of them expired with him and are now lost to us forever. Therefore, I am attempting to record this episode in his life as closely as I can remember his exact words, with some additional details about names and dates that I have taken from old newspapers.

Even in his old age, Steve was a big, hearty man with a huge port wine birthmark on the right side of his face. I was told he grew up in New York City and first shipped out of Fulton Market on one of the small sloops which operated out of there. At the turn of the century, Noank had the reputation of being the home port of many of the high-line fishermen and it is not surprising that an energetic young man with his eye on eventual command soon gravitated to a Noank schooner. Steve fitted right in for, from all accounts, he was known in his younger days as one of the strongest of the strong and among the hardiest of a whole breed of tough schoonermen. He earned a good portion of that reputation early-on as mate of Captain Silas Latham's schooner *ESTHER ANITA* during the gale of September 16, 1903. At the height of the storm, Captain Latham, Lewis Wilcox and Alfred Peat were washed overboard by a boarding sea and drowned. Steve was the only other man on deck at the time and was credited with singlehanded-ly saving the vessel from being sunk with all hands. Tragedy also struck other vessels that day, for a number of boats and quite a few lives were lost, including two more Noank men, Captain John Morgan and Ned Peterson, who were washed overboard from the schooner *M.A. BASTON.*

The *ESTHER ANITA* had been bluefishing off Fire Island on the Cholera Bank when the storm struck and, as was common in those days, was anchored on the grounds chumming with ground-up menhaden, which were used to attract the schools of bluefish to the boat so the crew could catch them with baited handlines. The weather had looked threatening at sunrise, with an increasing northeast wind and moderate rain, but everybody figured that it was just another one of the usual September storms they had to put up with each fall. The *ESTHER ANITA* was not the only boat on the Cholera Bank that fateful day, for several other schooners were in sight, also anchored up and bluefishing. None of the captains wanted to waste several days by running into New York at the first sign of a blow; better to tough it out by staying on the grounds and be ready to fish if it moderated the next day. In addition, a number of other perfectly good reasons made this a stan-dard practice, especially on the Cholera Bank. Foremost was the simple fact that, in the days before the invention of electronic navigational aids, it sometimes took two or three days of searching around to locate a particular rockpile on an off-shore bank. When you had finally found the one you were looking for and the fish were "On the Bite", you hung in there as long as you could. A secondary consid-eration in the reduced visibility of gale conditions, was the possibility of being run down by a steamer if you blundered into a shipping lane as you approached Ambrose Lightship. Lastly, but probably equally important, was the desire of almost all captains to keep their crew members away from the readily available "Temptations of the Flesh" prevalent along the New York waterfront, especially during the middle of a fishing trip.

The downside of this decision, which became the indirect cause of the three fatalities on the *ESTHER ANITA*, was the complete lack of power equipment on most of the fishing schooners. Up until it became readily available, sailing fisher-men were especially vulnerable when they anchored, for the manually operated windlasses bolted to their foredecks were simply not capable of retrieving a heavy fluke anchor and about 100 fathoms of 2-inch manila anchor warp if it finally got too rough to remain on the hook. At that point, there was only one way out; set a double reefed foresail to gather some way while, at the same time, a couple of the gang lashed the pennant of a marker buoy to the anchor cable between the bow and the bitt. The next step was to grab an axe, cut the cable at the bitt and hope to be able to find the buoy again after the storm abated. These were desperate measures for both the vessel and the men working on the exposed foredeck for there were a lot of things that could go wrong. The worst being the possibility of a breaking sea washing the crewmen off the bow.

As any avid salt water fisherman knows, bluefish always seem to feed heavily when a storm is brewing and, according to what Steve Bagnall told me, this is what took place that morning. The *ESTHER ANITA* was anchored on a big pile of bluefish that were biting furiously and the crew were "Mohawking" them (although probably politically incorrect today, the phrase is still in general use among rod and reel fishermen to indicate they are catching fish as fast as they can haul them in). As the morning wore on, the wind and waves steadily increased and the surging of the schooner against the bowstring taut anchor cable was making it very difficult to work on deck. Captain Latham had put down his best anchor on a new warp. Soon it became too rough to work on deck in safety and the wind was blowing so hard the crew was unable to haul the anchor with the windlass. By this time, everyone was soaked to the skin so Captain Latham let all but a few of the crew retire to the forecastle to drip-dry and warm up. Several of the crewmen were very concerned about the situation, but Captain Latham assured them he had laid at anchor in a lot worse weather and the *ESTHER ANITA* had rode it out in fine order.

However, in a very short time the wind increased to hurricane force and the seas, which before had been large but not a deadly threat to the vessel, began breaking over the bow with alarming frequency. It became clear the immense strain on the anchor cable was not allowing the ships bow to rise and "give" with the waves as well as it would have if it were free of the restraining anchor. By this time, the crew sheltered in the focsle out of the weather, were urging Captain Latham to cut the anchor cable and get the schooner underway so they could either heave-to under reefed canvass or jog inshore under the lee of Gravesend Bay. According to Steve Bagnall, in spite of the rapidly deteriorating weather, it was obvious that Captain Latham, who had a well deserved reputation for being ultra conservative when it came to spending money, was simply not going to cut away a new warp and his best anchor if he thought they would survive at anchor.

Steve Bagnall, Captain Silas Latham, Lewis Wilcox and Alfred Peat were the only ones who remained on deck and had tackled the difficult job of tying a triple reef in the doused but still wildly flapping foresail. When finished, they refurled it to the boom with a bare minimum of lashings so it could be hoisted quickly if the anchor line parted. Lewis Wilcox and Steve were discussing their perilous situation and trying to convince Captain Latham to buoy and cut the anchor warp when they saw a huge breaking sea bearing down on the bow of the laboring schooner. Captain Latham ran aft to the wheel and grabbed the spokes to brace himself. Steve yelled to the others "JUMP" and, leaping up, grasped the main boom and wrapped himself tightly around it. The other two men, being rather short of stature and lacking Steve's size and athletic ability, apparently thought their best chance would be to hang onto the main rigging and remained standing on deck.

The waves that day were described in newspaper accounts of the storm as being "mountain high", and so they must have been. When that big breaker came roaring down the length of the deck, it twisted the focsle hatch askew, snatched the bait seine from amidships, washed Captain Silas Latham from the wheel, entangled him in the twine and swept man and seine away, never more to be seen. At the same time Lewis Wilcox and Alfred Peat were torn from their places at the main shrouds and followed Captain Latham over the stern, leaving Steve Bagnall alone on deck, clinging to the boom. For a few moments, the two crewmen could be seen struggling in the water astern but, the ship being at anchor, there was nothing Steve could do to save them.

His immediate concern was for the safety of the ship and the rest of her men, as it was pretty certain that another couple of waves like the last one would be the end for them all. Dropping to the deck, he raced forward, sliced the lashings securing the foresail to the boom and gaff, and grabbed the peak and throat halyards together. With what must have been the strength of desperation, in a few tremendous heaves, he somehow managed to hoist them enough to get the sail to draw. As the boat slowly began to make headway he grabbed a hatchet and, with a single blow, severed the anchor line. Pausing not even a second, he raced aft again and threw the lashings off the wheel to keep the schooner from bearing off too far and getting broadside to the seas. By the time the rest of the crew had managed to force their way through the jammed focsle hatch, Steve had the vessel under control and jogging toward New York Harbor and safety.

Even today, I get the chills as I relive this event in my mind's eye. I can still see Steve's disfigured face and remember vividly his deep, curiously accented voice with its admixture of New York and Yankee speech patterns and wish once again I had made the effort to write down Steve's story of the storm at the time he related it because contemporary newspaper accounts of the tragedy are rather brief and very sketchy as to the details. However, the essential facts of the story I heard from Steve Bagnall over 50 years ago, jibe completely with what I read on microfilm in the New London Library.

Schooner ESTHER ANITA, *built Essex, Mass. 1898. Schooner saved by Steve Bagnall during storm. Photo courtesy of Robert S. Palmer.*

Chapter Eleven

WATERFRONT MEMORIES

As I began to write this assortment of reminiscences about my youth in what Theodore Dreiser described in his book *TWELVE MEN* as a "washed up little fishing village," I cannot help communicating how lucky I was to be born and brought up in such a unique and historically conscious area. Why I became a fisherman instead of the dentist my mother had hoped I would become is uncertain. I do know, at one time it seemed it was just plain ill fortune that forced me to help my Dad aboard the family boat, but now I am not so sure. It might even have been predestination, in the genes so to speak. I really never thought of it in that light until I did some research into my Dad's family tree and found that, in nine out of the ten generations since my ancestors settled Block Island, my direct male line had been either fishermen or seamen. It sort of makes you wonder, doesn't it?

Looking around Noank's waterfront as we approach the next century, it often seems to me that the memories of my boyhood are not only of another time, but of a different place. The nearly gentrified scene that is thought by tourists to be quaint, bears only a superficial resemblance to what I remember it being in my youth. For one thing, except for Ford's Lobsters, it is almost completely sanitized and the majority of the junk and debris have been removed. The docks are now kept in good repair and there are no more decaying fisherman's shacks perched precariously along the shore. Not so in the 1930s, 40s and even the early 50s, when there were one or more commercial fishboat docks and a small fleet of wooden draggers coming in most every night to take out their catch. There was also a straggly line of the now forbidden oak stakes running along the edge of the flats, which today are jammed with moorings for the fiberglass sailboats that crowd just about all the harbors in New England. Although a few of the stakes were regularly used by fishermen who could not find space at a dock, most were used only in case of stormy weather, or when you were not going to be fishing for a long time.

My earliest memories of the waterfront begin in the mid 1930s, and due no doubt to my tender age, are centered around our Riverview Avenue home. At that time Erastus "Rat" Wilbur was operating at least one of the fish-houses. Ray Coon had a fish market on the town dock and "Rat's" son in law, Walt MacDonald, was running the fish dock at the foot of Latham Lane. The most deteriorated of the docks being used by the boats was right in front of our house where Chip and Freddy Anderson's dock is today and, although still being used by a few of the smaller draggers, it was definitely on its last legs. From a tourism standpoint, you would have to say the view from our front windows was certainly picturesque, for there was an almost totally rotten dock and a decaying fish packing house which included a so-called office and a large ice storage room. The building was supported on one end by the shore, but the remainder extended over the water and was held up by shipworm infested pilings which appeared ready to collapse into the river at any moment. Northeast of the dock (called *Up-River* by us locals) were two 2500 gallon cylindrical steel gasoline tanks perched precariously on top of a 10-foot high wood cribbing made from 6x6 timbers. *Up-River* from the fuel tanks was a one and a half story storage building that leaned to the north about 15 degrees. The storage shed had, at some time in the distant past, been painted yellow which was now laced with brown streaks from the rusty nails in the sheathing. The crib and gas tanks were originally painted a dark green, which was peeling badly. Except for some signs concerning the business formerly occupying the premises, the fish packing house had never known the touch of a paintbrush. As a small child, I can remember my mother saying she wished the owners of the property would either fix the buildings up or tear them down. She got her wish all right, but not in the way she intended. Regional waterfront redevelopment, in the guise of the 1938 hurricane, cleaned up this conglomeration in the course of one very long September afternoon and piled the whole shooting match on our front yards and roads, changing forever the character of this part of the village.

Not only was the waterfront in front of our house in a run-down condition, but you only had to look towards Morgan Point to see Noank Shipyard with its melange of decaying wooden watercraft. These included, among many others, the 4-masted schooner *ALICE L. PENDELTON*, the beam trawlers *ALBATROSS* and *FISH HAWK* (whose pilot house is now a cottage on Morgan Point) plus the menhaden steamers *STEVEN McKEVER* and *ANNIE L. WILCOX*. In addition to the abandoned boats at the Shipyard, there was a red-painted steel yacht, about 80 feet long, aboard which a mysterious foreigner and his equally mysterious female companion lived for several years. The local scuttlebutt had it that he was suspected of being a German spy and the huge radio antenna strung between the masts on his yacht did nothing to allay those opinions. As well as I can remember, he just disappeared shortly after war was declared and someone towed the yacht away.

Most of the boats in "dead" storage at Noank Shipyard were removed when the yard was rejuvenated during World War II and construction of several wooden minesweepers began. Unfortunately, after completing only two, no further contracts were forthcoming and the workforce was laid off. The property was soon sold to a Mr. Townsend who operated some sort of marine salvage and shipbreaking business in the New York area. Unfortunately, he used the yard for storing salvaged or surplus boats while dismantling them for scrap. One of the first to arrive was the 4-masted schooner *ANNIE* which was reported to have been used as a floating barracks, had somehow sunk and was raised by Townsend. True to form, it very shortly sank again from lack of care and rolled over on her side in front of where Wes Maxwell's docks are now. Not content with that unsightly mess, he then imported an old wooden lightship and what was reputed to be Holland's original submarine. He cut the sub up for scrap and the lightship ended up on the northeast end of "Ahoy" Island after the 1944 hurricane. As an explanation for those unfamiliar with local history, the two small islands to the northeast of Ram Island do not have officially recognized names, but Arthur Henry, who built a house on the middle islet in the late 1800s, named his island "Quirk" and the other one "Ahoy". Henry's island is still referred to locally as "Quirk" and in the absence of any actual name, I have decided to continue using Henry's name for the other island.

Shortly after the end of the war, Townsend brought Noank's waterfront two more gifts in the form of a pair of war surplus LSTs which he proceeded to cut up for scrap with the assistance of a group of very questionable characters who were housed in one of the Shipyard buildings. Around the time the second LST had been nearly reduced to scrap, two of the roustabouts got in a fight in the barracks one night, a not unusual event according to local gossip. However, this time a gun was involved and the looser wound up dead. The murder seemed to put a damper on work in the Shipyard and soon the Townsend shipbreaking activities

The Derelict lightship brought to Noank Shipyard by Townsend and blown over to "Ahoy" Island by the 1944 hurricane. Burned by parties unknown V.J. night, August 5, 1945. Arnold Crossman (kneeling) and John Rathbun (standing) on bow of derelict lightship off "Ahoy" Island, late 1944.

ground to a halt until the yard was purchased by Don Singer. As for the lightship, it stayed aground on the end of "Ahoy" Island for several years, listing at about a 20 degree angle, and then burned to the water's edge when it caught fire from what was officially reported as "Spontaneous Combustion" on V-J night August 5, 1945. In spite of persistent rumors involving me in the caper, they are absolutely untrue and, furthermore, I have kept faith all these years with my promise not to reveal the actual culprits.

While I am not going to compile a list of all the many commercial fishermen and boats who worked out of our port during my formative years, I do want to mention Noank's last sailing fishermen. They were an incredibly hardy breed (many were from Nova Scotia) who tub-trawled for tilefish from dories launched from Grover Eldridge's schooner RELIANCE before the war and his schooner BLACK HAWK afterwards. When the BLACK HAWK ceased operation after the death of Grover Eldridge, it was truly the end of the age of commercial sail in this part of New England. Nearly all of the dorymen and dragger men I knew in those days were full-time commercial fishermen working year-round at their trade. This is indeed a far cry from today, when the majority of our fishermen are forced to depend on a shore side job for most of their income. Not to say this is a bad thing, but it does reflect the tenor of the present times and the sad state of the inshore bottom trawl fishery.

Vivid images of a few isolated childhood incidents connected with the shore still remain as fresh in my mind as the day they took place. They include Millard DeBiasi diving overboard to save Artie MacDonald's life when he was knocked unconscious by hitting his head as he fell off "Rat" Wilbur's dock; Lauren Ellis's boat IDELLA catching fire from a gasoline explosion; an 8-year old boy (me) trudging down to the Town Dock with a wooden bucket to get it filled with 20 pounds of bait squid from Ray Coon's fishmarket and then struggling home with it clutched to my chest because I was not tall enough to carry it by the becket; and lastly, my brother John falling overboard from my Dad's boat and me tossing that same wooden bucket to him for a life preserver, until my Dad could fish him out.

Standing head and shoulders above these events and ranking second only to my memories of the 1938 hurricane, is my Dad and Mom standing on the shore shooting at a dockline on a 30 foot open motor launch during a storm. This unlikely event took place around 1936, in the midst of a September gale, at the dock in front of our house and was the talk of the waterfront for days afterward. It happened like this. The launch, I believe it was owned by Gerard Laffargue, was tied up on the northeast side of the dock, facing to the southeast, when the wind shifted to the southwest and, as it often does, really began to blow. I don't know why it is, but these southerly storms always seem to be at their height at the top of the tide, and it was certainly no exception on that day. To make matters worse, the storm tide and big seas had torn away the rotten planks leading from the shore to the main part of the dock and isolated the boat. Six or eight local fishermen, along with the owner of the launch, had come down to the shore and were huddled between the overhead gasoline tanks and the fish packing house to see what, if anything, could be done about the boat's desperate situation. The launch was rolling her rails under with every wave and, unless the weather moderated, it looked like it would be only a matter of time before the boat would either roll over or sink from the water crashing over the sides as it thrashed about.

The general consensus among the gang was that, unless the stern line parted and allowed the launch to swing around and ride head-to-sea, it would be a goner. "I betcha I could shoot that line off with my 22 bolt action Savage," my Dad told them. The crew all had a good laugh at that for the line was jerking all around and only was still for a very brief moment when it was under the most strain. "Jees-us Benny, whatcha think you are, Buffalo Bill or somethin," one of his friends commented to the delight of the others, most of whom considered the remark to be a real thigh slapper. My Dad didn't say anything in reply to the outburst, but just stood there watching the boat gyrate for a few moments, then turned around and headed up the driveway towards our house. "Where ya goin Benny?" someone said. "Gonna get my rifle," my old man replied, as he plodded through the wind and spray toward the house. In a few minutes he was back, along with my Mom who had tagged along to watch the proceedings. My Dad was actually known to be a crack shot, for he belonged to the Morgan Rifle League and competed regularly on one of their target teams. Not only that, he had a mini target-range set up in our dirt cellar where he, my Mom and both my brother John and I practiced on a regular basis. However, hitting a small, snapping, vibrating line at 30 yards in the midst of a 55 knot gale was hardly anything one could practice doing on a rifle range or in a dirt-cellar that had only about 4 feet of headroom.

My Dad brought along a full box of 22-long bullets, as even the most optimistic marksman would realize a couple of 5 shot clips would not be enough for the job facing him that day. He loaded up the clip and got ready to give it a go. The prone position, which would give the most chance of a steady aim, was out of the question on the steep down-slope of the shoreline, so he tried the first couple of shots from a kneeling stance. This tactic didn't work out at all, for the strong cross-wind buffeted him so much he couldn't even come close to hitting the line during the split second it was stretched tight. He then stood up, moved over to the framework holding the overhead gasoline tanks and, using that as a brace, steadied down on the place where the line would be when it was under extreme tension. By this time, the group of bystanders had grown larger and more good natured bantering started between my Dad and some of his friends. Finally he told them to "Cut it out!" so he could concentrate on the task at hand, but this comment only intensified the ribbing he was taking about what looked to them to be an impossible undertaking.

To the obvious delight of the group, my Dad proceeded to fire off two clips of ammunition without any noticeable effect on the stern line. "Maybe you shud-a brought two boxes of shells," quipped one of the more persistent kibitzers. My old man just ignored him as he squeezed off another shot and, low and behold, a sizeable chunk of the line flew into the air. This certainly quieted the snide comments from the group and a few of them gathered round to congratulated the proud marksman. Some of the others were still unconvinced and a couple of them muttered that it was just fool luck. "Ya got lucky that time Benny," said one of them. "Lets see ya knock off the rest of the rope before we pat ya on the back." My dad had zeroed in on the target by this time and, after squeezing off another two clips of ammunition, managed to hit the line again and parted one of the three strands.

As he was reloading the clip from the box of shells my Mom was holding open for him, he asked her if she would like to take a couple of shots. She just laughed and shook her head no. He didn't say anything in reply, shrugged his shoulders, steadied himself up against the cribbing and squinted along the sights. By this time, the wind had picked up even more than before and it was blowing at least 60 knots. The rain was hammering down and the boat was nearly obscured in the spume. This definitely affected my Dad's marksmanship, for three 5-shot clips went down the drain before he had another hit and took out about half of one of the two remaining strands. Even his most severe critics had come over to his side by now, but the box of shells was beginning to get low and, while he was reloading, my Mom asked him if he would like to have her get another full box from the house.

He didn't reply to her at all, but just continued to stuff the last 2 cartridges into the clip. "Darn rain's getting my good rifle all soaked," he said to nobody in particular as he handed the reloaded piece to my Mom. "Here," he announced in a tone that was more of an order than a request, "It's your turn now Anna." My Mom didn't protest or even utter a word in reply; she simply took the rifle and steadied it against the upright timber. A long time seemed to go by and she had not even made a first shot for practice. "What-sa matter Anna, got buck fever?" bantered one of our good friends. "Shaddup you clown," said my Dad "she's just getting it timed." About that time there was the crack of a shot, most of the remaining two strands of the rope went flying into the air, the boat heaved up on top of a comber and what was left of the final strand let go with a loud POP.

The rest was anticlimactic; the boat swung around with her bow to the seas and now rode easily, everybody congratulated my parents, especially my Mom, and my Dad took a chorus of ribbing from all his buddies about her one-shot success. "You shud-a let her do it from the start and you would-a saved a lot of ammunition, Benny," was all he heard for days afterward from his friends.

Dock and location where my Mom shot line off boat.

I suppose it is human nature to avoid thinking of oneself as such, but it's becoming distressingly obvious that I have become an "Old Timer" even though I tend to view myself within the same mental framework I had during high school. Technically speaking, a strict definition of this term is still probably well beyond the capabilities of the finest intellects. Nevertheless, it would seem you are fast approaching the state of marine old-timership as soon as most of your fellow skippers have never even heard of someone who was a world-class highliner when you were a youth. I certainly had no inkling I would ever attain such a dubious distinction when I shipped out as a junior stern man on my father's lobsterboat in late May of 1942. Now shipped out, although it has a distinctly nautical ring to it, is a bit of an overstatement and the unvarnished truth is much more prosaic. What really happened went something like this. In 1942, at breakfast one spring morning my mother calmly announced that, seeing as I was going to graduate from Noank Grammar School in June and my dad would be needing some help on the boat come summer, I was going to be "IT"; end of discussion.

The spring of 1942 was only a few months after the Japanese attack on Pearl Harbor and local rumor had it that President Roosevelt felt the German Navy might attempt to launch a commando-type attack on the Submarine Base or Electric Boat Shipyard from the U-boats which were already torpedoing merchant vessels within sight of Long Island. The danger, remote though it may have been in reality, was actually of great concern to our military planners and, in order to enhance the "Security" of the Port of New London, they imposed a series of restrictions on marine commerce, fishermen included. This meant that all commercial fishermen would be required to register with the Captain of the Port's office and get a so-called Port Security card which they had to have on their person when on the water (sort of a marine drivers license). For many, especially those of us still underage, it was our first exposure to the mug shots and fingerprinting that have become so common in government and industry today.

Because the presumed German threat to the installations on the Groton shore of the Thames river required the special registration for commercial fishermen to be completed before we could haul our lobster pots, my Dad and I took the bus to New London at the first opportunity. We got out at the Parade and walked from there to Fort Trumbull where his lifelong friend, Robert P. Anderson, Sr. was serving as Captain of the Port for New London. As for using the bus and walking all the way to Ft. Trumbull from downtown New London, even if we owned a car, which we didn't, we probably would have done that to save our precious gas ration stamps. Once there and escorted by the guard to the Captain of the Port's office, we filled out the necessary forms, which looked complicated to us, but would be considered quite simple today, submitted our birth certificates for examination, got fingerprinted and sat for our pictures. I, for one, had the very uncomfortable feeling that I was about to lose my anonymity and would, from this day forward, be on Uncle Sam's list. The feeling was immediately reinforced by the Yeoman processing our applications, who calmly announced to us that all the personal information he had received from us was going to be forwarded to the FBI in Washington. Boy, being registered with the U.S. Coast Guard was actually not too disturbing a thought, but the realization that my photo and finger-prints were to be examined and filed away for future reference by J. Edgar Hoover's G-Men, was a shock of the first magnitude.

I guess all the fishermen present that day were found to be stable patriotic U.S. citizens, for I never heard of anybody getting a visit from the Feds. This opinion is reinforced by the plain fact that, among a group of local fishermen, something of this importance could never have occurred without the whole fleet being aware of it within 20 or 30 minutes, at the most. At any rate, we were all certified as commercial fishermen and were issued a laminated plastic Port Security card, picture and all, that looked a lot like our present Motor Vehicle drivers license. I still have the card which depicts a rather dopey looking kid who appears to be either dazed or intoxicated and obviously not bright enough to be a spy or an enemy agent.

The boats were also registered at the same time and given a three letter identification and required to fly the international code flags denoting those letters from the rigging whenever they were underway. This was OK, but in typical bureaucratic fashion, in which nothing can be simple and straightforward, the Coast Guard decided security would be greatly enhanced if these code letters were changed every 30 days. This "Hoist" as it was called by the Coast Guard, meant the boat-owner had to either buy a complete set of very expensive (at least to us) international signal flags or sew them up as needed. Being Yankees, we naturally did the latter and my mother was immediately promoted to official flag manufacturer. Betsy Ross she was not, nor did we always have cloth of the exact color required, but the U.S. Coast Guard never seemed to mind, so I guess the flags passed muster.

Chapter Twelve

NOANK GRAMMAR SCHOOL

Noank Grammar School. Photo: Noank Historical Society, Inc.

School was certainly a lot different when I was growing up. It's not that we wrote with charcoal on slate by the light of a kerosene lantern, as some of the present generation might think, but our so-called "learning experience" started and finished on a much different note from today's schools. I also was doubly fortunate in going to Noank Grammar School (now called Noank Elementary School) which, at that time, had a combined 6th, 7th and 8th grade ruled over by a truly remarkable middle aged woman known then as Mrs. Mary Virginia Morgan. Mrs. Morgan, who unfortunately would not last a week under the present politically and socially correct rules for teacher conduct, had extraordinary teaching ability and a lifelong interest in classical literature. Although not directly connected with this story, even today her personal life would be considered unconventional. Not only was she an avowed Democrat in a staunchly Republican bastion, where Democrats were considered in the same context with Bolshevik revolutionaries, but her first two husbands were many years older than she. As a parent who raised two girls, I cannot even guess what her family thought when, at 28 years of age, she married 82 year old Deacon Roswell Sawyer, who subsequently lived to the ripe old age of 93. Within a year of Deacon Sawyer's death, she took husband number two, Deacon Agustus V. Morgan, age 79 or 80 who, 5 years later, left her a widow for the second time. She then remained unmarried for many years until, late in life, she married John Goodman, a man her own age, but unfortunately he died within a year.

Mrs. Goodman, who eventually had the title of "The Duchess of Noank" bestowed on her (perhaps by herself), was far and away the most influential teacher I was privileged to have studied under. She came from a family whose forebears had been among the earliest settlers in Groton and was interested in and very knowledgeable about U.S. and local history. During the three years in which we were under her control-there was absolutely no doubt in either her mind or ours as to this-she taught us a great deal about early colonial history. Of equal importance, she had the rare ability to stimulate her pupils' interest in learning more about the subject. History, however, was merely an offshoot of her abiding respect for the classics and, because she knew that no normal 6th graders would willingly tackle classical literature by themselves, she read it to us. She had an extremely expressive speaking voice, a firm command of the King's English and a demeanor that would have done credit to a U.S. Senator. Furthermore, she definitely did not brook inattention to what she was reading or saying, not from her students, nor from whomever she was addressing at any time in her long productive life. She read us most of Shakespeare, Robert Burns, Victor Hugo and several other classical authors, plus excerpts from Longfellow, Whittier and Robert Frost among other poets before we graduated from eighth grade. It might be called force feeding, but we digested a lot more of it than you would imagine.

There were other differences in grade school between my youth and now besides the educational aspects. Take recess for instance. I am not sure just what it is called today, probably something bland like "Supervised Physical Activity", but to me it will always be "Recess". Back then the only supervision occurred after the fact and usually consisted of stopping nosebleeds, applying a band-aid to a minor cut, or trying to sort out who had started the fight or had broken one of the few unwritten rules that were understood to be in force. It goes without saying there was no school nurse within miles. Short of a compound fracture of the femur or being knocked unconscious for more than 15 minutes, you were pretty much on your own when it came to relatively minor injuries. Of course, if the wound appeared likely to distract the class, you were sent home so your parents could patch you up, as these things were considered to be their responsibility and not the school's. Sue the school system over Johnny's missing front tooth, you gotta be kidding! I am fairly sure that some of the teachers must have glanced out now and then to see if any major catastrophe had taken place, but in the main they had recess from us as well.

One thing which is probably never going to change was the girls and boys separated themselves during recess into groups segregated by sex. The girls to do whatever young girls everywhere do, and the boys to play whatever pickup game was possible. Which game we played was usually determined by only two factors. The first by the usual male peer dominance, with the larger boys deciding things for the group, and the second by who had brought what to play with. The Groton School Board felt we were there to LEARN and therefore provided no playground equipment of any type for the Noank Grammar School. As a matter of fact, it came as a bit of a cultural shock when I got to Fitch High School and was exposed to an organized sports program with gym classes and group hot water showers. Up to then, my only contact with running hot water was at my grandparents' home in Norwich, where they had a bathtub, but no shower. At our house on Riverview Avenue, we were still washing-up at the kitchen sink using water heated in a big copper teakettle.

At a typical Noank Grammar School "Recess" the two major team games were touch football and a form of baseball played with a sponge rubber ball, using your arm and clenched fist for a bat. The reason for only touch football was that the schoolyard was paved with stony gravel mixed with yellow dirt, so tackle football was banned by the principal and, more importantly, by almost all parents. As for baseball, the small size of the fenced school yard naturally precluded the use of a bat for Noank's version of the national pastime. Abner Doubleday definitely would not have been proud of us. Very poor field conditions were only the first of many impediments to playing a proper game of baseball for our diamond would have looked right at home in the comic strip BC. Home plate was a flat rock we stored near the well house; first base was a steel post in the middle the chain link fence; second base was a telephone pole that the power company had thoughtfully planted right in the middle of the yard; and third was usually another flat rock kept near the building foundation. I say usually, because every so often the town would send a work crew over to pick up the yard and then it was bye-bye to third base.

Needless to say, the fact that all four bases were hard and/or immovable objects and numerous small to medium sized rocks stuck out of the packed gravel, sliding to beat the throw was not a prudent move. The only base that was even remotely safe to slide into was first where continual scuffing had worn a depression that left about a 6 inch high by 2 feet long gap under the twisted steel wires on the bottom of the fence. To this day, most all of the local boys who grew up with me still have one or two long furrowed scars on their legs made by these wires when they happened to slide a little too wide or far. This was both painful and embarrassing for the wires would bend out slightly when you slammed into them. If you then became tightly wedged you were unable to pull away without jamming the points even deeper into your anatomy. When this took place, one or two of your buddies, who always seemed to consider your predicament hilariously funny, would have to run out the front gate, down the outside of the fence and pull it up and out to free you from its grasp. You also learned very quickly that it was crucial to your physical well-being to keep your legs TOGETHER when you slid into first or, God forbid, into second base. At first base you had the fence to stop you before the post reached your crotch, but at second you also had to remember to slide high so that if your feet missed the base you only bounced your butt off the telephone pole and didn't incur serious harm to several extremely sensitive parts of your body.

Another semi-organized physical activity for the older boys was a type of mayhem that we called WARREE, which was a local variation of a game commonly known as "King of the Hill." Playing WARREE was frowned on by the teachers and it went through periodic cycles of being forbidden, usually when someone was hurt seriously enough to require major medical attention. However, like all forbidden activity left unsupervised, it would gradually return, until another casualty occurred. Frankly, from my adult perspective, I hesitate to call WARREE a game, unless running back a kickoff without the help of downfield blockers or protective equipment would meet your criteria. Whatever the definition, it was what would be called an "Action" sport today, for there were next to no rules and participating was simplicity itself. We usually "played" east and west across the front of the schoolyard (which today is Noank Park) from one chainlink fence to the other. The game normally began with the time honored ritual of designating someone to be "IT", either by an older boy ordering a smaller boy to volunteer or, more often, by narrowing the choices down to two. The pair would then go fist-over-fist up a ball bat or stick until the loser could no longer get enough of a grip to keep it from falling.

After we had coerced someone into being IT, everyone else (usually 15 to 20 guys and occasionally a few tomboy-type girls) lined up along the east fence, leaving the one who was IT in the middle. At a signal from one of the older boys, everybody yelled out WARREE at the top of their lungs and charged full tilt toward the opposite side. The boy in the middle then attempted to grab and hold someone, preferably without resorting to a tackle and, when successful, there would be two kids guarding the middle on the next charge. Actually being chosen, or forced, to be IT was probably the safest position to play, for usually a friend or two would allow you to capture them fairly easily. They could then assist you to gang-up on someone you were trying to get even with. Aha, you say; now you know why it was often banned.

However, the first part of the so-called game was sort of fun and generally pretty safe, with most everyone being reasonably careful about things. But, boys being boys, after almost all of the "Players" were in the middle trying to hang on to one or two survivors, both the survivors and the mob in the middle had been elbowed and kicked often enough that the more aggressive types had long since lost whatever cool they started with. If you were lucky or a very tough kid who would beat the tar out of someone who intentionally used the game as an excuse to beat up on you, you escaped with only a few bumps and bruises. Others were not as lucky. I remember that one of the first things John Bates did when he became principal was to absolutely forbid WARREE.

However, being a thoroughly fair minded administrator, he did what no teacher had ever done before at Noank Grammar School. He bought us an inflated rubber kickball with his own money and instituted a little supervision at recess. Being new, and therefore interesting, we dove into the sport of kick baseball with enthusiasm. It certainly had some advantages over the form of fist ball we had been playing. For one thing, if you have ever swung at a semi-soft rubber ball with all your might when the pitcher threw you what could be charitably described as an inside fastball and the ball connected with the soft part of your wrist just above your hand, you know how it feels. It HURTS LIKE HELL for a long time. It's no wonder so many of us grew up with cramped handwriting.

The kickball itself led a very hard life and quickly accumulated a lot of patches as a result of hitting the sharp twisted wires on the top of the chain link fence. Although we all tried hard to prevent this, very often it would carom off someone, catch the top of the fence and tear another hole in the rubber. After recess, Mr. Bates would take the wounded ball over to Ray Coon at the gas station across the street and have an innertube patch put on. I have no doubt that over the course of a school year, "Coonie," as he was known, spent as much time patching the poor kickball as he did flat tires.

The west fence was not the only drawback to our new playground game. Because the main entrance to the schoolyard bisected our kickball playing field at a right angle, we also had to be on guard against smacking any innocent bystanders who blundered into range of a kicked ball. Fellow pupils knew enough to keep out of harms way and to look both ways before crossing what passed for our court, but the teachers and visiting parents were inclined to assume we were keeping a lookout and would wander right across the "Infield". This was especially true of Mrs. Mary Virginia Morgan, who always assumed she had the right of way over any student playground activity and totally ignored our ball game as she stalked purposefully from the gate to the schoolhouse.

Eighth grade class, Noank Grammar School, 1942. Front row, left to right: Valentino Giommi, Benjamin Rathbun, Colleen Sullivan, Kathleen Valentine (Burdick), Mary Mitchell, Donald Phillips, Patsy Piacenza.
Second row, left to right: Teacher Mary Virginia Morgan, Charles Thompson, Hugh Smyth, Norris Fish, Bernard Carson, Harold Foster, Principal John S. Bates.

All went well until the day when Patsy Piacenza nailed her in the right temple with a line drive that knocked one of her famous French hats half way to the west fence. Talk about your death rays; her eyes swept the group with such intensity that, I swear, scraps of paper burst into flame and the grass on the adjoining yard withered and died. We were all cowering in fear of what her next move would be. I'm sure Patsy's life flashed before his mind's eye, as he fully expected to be subject to a fate vastly worse than death, whatever that might be. However, nothing untoward happened to any of us, due in great part to the fact we all carefully avoided direct eye contact with her for fear of being struck blind. Like most of my generation, we had been told that peeking at a girl when she was unclothed might cause blindness and had been cautioned by the older boys to make sure we covered one eye if such a chance arose. The kickball incident was obviously even more dangerous than viewing a naked teenager. Fortunately for our future eyesight, our group escaped with only two cases of pinkeye, one sty and a prohibition on the use of the kickball for a solid week.

Another activity usually limited to boys under the age of puberty was seeing how high you could pee (puberty being the age that sexual shyness between males suddenly begins to raise its head). The ritual was rooted in antiquity, or so the kindergarten pupils were given to understand by the older boys, and took place in the unheated outhouse attached to the west end of the janitor's workshop located at the north end of the schoolyard; the girls outhouse being on the east end. I was never bold enough to venture into the girls part, but the boys section was a typical 3-holer with a high-backed sheet metal trough running across one end. These were true outhouses and, like all real privies, had no running water and depended on the regular application of chloride of lime to keep the "vapors" down to a tolerable level; at least that was the theory. The theory worked OK in the winter, but on a hot June day often failed to perform up to community standards, especially if the janitor, Steve Bagnall, had used up his yearly lime allowance. While a 3-hole school outhouse might be a distinct cultural shock to most American youngsters today, it was not a big deal to us as the majority of us were still using an outhouse at home.

The peeing contest was an ongoing event at every recess and, if more than one boy was at the trough, was considered a mandatory activity. However, as in all sporting events, in order to excel at this fiercely competitive bodily function, it was necessary to employ some rudimentary tactics. As a matter of fact, among males of my generation having to "go" during class was considered to be a mark of weakness by your peers and was only utilized in dire emergencies. You first had to get the attention of the teacher by raising your hand, which was no mean feat with several of the stricter types who didn't care to be interrupted. The teacher would pause; "Yesss, Mr. (or Miss) so and so. What do you want?" as if she didn't already know. By this time every eye in the room was on you as you stammered your request to "leave the room". The phrase was also traditional. No local kid ever asked to go to the bathroom, possibly because some of us had only a vague knowledge of what a bathroom really was. The boys would all grin at your embarrassment and look at you with that "What a weenie" expression as you tried to get out of the room as quickly as possible.

In addition, the natural tendency to visit the outhouse as soon as class let out for recess was considered to be the mark of a sissy. No boy involved in the peeing competition "went" during class or recess until it was absolutely impossible to hold out another moment. That way you gained the advantage of having maximum pressure to give you greatly increased height. It also had the added benefit of teaching me the ironclad bladder control necessary for success as a charterboat skipper who often cannot leave the helm when the fish are biting. While skill in the conventional sports earned a measure of fame among ones peers, at Noank Grammar School, those who could pee higher than their heads were considered to be in an athletic class by themselves.

Another ritual we were forced to participate in was the line-up out in the playground when the bell rang at the end of recess. This took place fair weather and foul, with much more speed and precision in foul. The only thing actually required was to line up in two columns in some semblance of order and SHUT UP. Lining up was OK, but to think a bunch of kids could keep quiet for several minutes during all the pushing and shoving that inevitably went on is stretching reality. Many teachers would just let the requirement for relative quiet pass and give us the go-ahead to troop back into the classroom. Others, Mrs. Mary Virginia Morgan in particular, were not as lenient. She would stand silently at the upstairs window with her arms folded across her bosom and her piercing eyes staring daggers down at us. To all but the most foolhardy, this was enough to shock us into comparative silence and acceptable behavior but, as they say, fools rush in where angels fear to tread.

When this took place, woe betide those who through exuberance or defiance had persisted in misbehaving, for then she would give several sharp raps on the window pane with her knuckle and point toward the offending child. You could almost see lightning bolts blast from her fingertip straight to the now cringing moppet who was most definitely in big "Do-Do". Although it very rarely happened, one series of raps and finger pointing was sometimes not enough to restore order and she would then launch another assault on the glass. When this happened it was Danger City for the entire class as, three times out of four, she would then tattoo the glass hard enough to break it right out of the frame. Although all of us knew enough to keep a straight face when the shards of glass tinkled down the stuccoed side of the building, some unfortunate wretch would inevitably burst out laughing. This was probably the worst move anyone could possibly make, for she considered laughing at her to be ridicule, a degree of freedom not open to anybody, let alone a lowly student.

Surprisingly, the line-up became less of a hassle when we reached the upper grades for by then the contempt of small boys for mere girls, and vice-versa, had slowly changed to intense curiosity and interest. The smaller kids always spaced themselves out when in line but, as we approached puberty and our sex hormones began to make themselves felt, our priorities suddenly shifted. Instead of trying to keep away from the girls when on line, our objectives flipped 180 degrees and we jockeyed for position in order to pack ourselves tightly against the more developed girls, especially in the warmer months when coats were no longer required. It was not really an overt act, but more of a sneaky shuffle so you wound up in front of a nubile young thing, who would then find that the front of her body with its budding little protuberances would be slowly squashed tightly against your back. It is a measure of our naivety that many of us were surprised when this new game turned out to be a lot more satisfying than hitting a home run or peeing higher than your head.

I guess, by today's standards, our primary school education would be rated as rather deficient culturally and definitely out of line as to discipline which, most of the time, was administered in full view of the entire class by whacking the flat side of an 18 inch ruler on the outstretched palms of the offenders. When the teacher ordered you to STAND UP AND HOLD OUT YOUR HANDS you knew you were in for it. At that point, the only question in your mind was how many whacks she was going to give you and could you keep from crying in front of your classmates. My brother, who had lightning-fast reflexes, but seemed to attract trouble without even trying, once managed to snatch the ruler away from Mrs. Hattie Fish on the first whack and was waving it around threateningly before order was finally restored.

Mrs. Morgan, on the other hand, never ran into that sort of problem for she could pistol-whip her charges into quivering submission using only her steely gaze and cutting sarcasm. A typical tongue-lashing went along these lines. She ordered you to march up to the front of the classroom and you had to stand there silently facing her for what seemed like forever while she stared intently at you. She could have given intimidation lessons to a Marine drill sergeant for an almost visible cloak of invincibility surrounded her on these occasions. She was absolutely certain she was fully in charge at all times and, as a soon to be punished student, you knew it right down to your little tippy-toes.

Most of the boys gladly would have suffered the momentary pain of the ruler to the scathing ridicule we knew was going to be administered to us in front of our friends and classmates, such as the following. "Young man, why don't you use some of your God-given brains once in awhile? That was an irresponsible way to act; I know you were brought up better than that and your mother will be SO ASHAMED of you if it is brought to her attention. From the way you've been behaving, you don't seem to have even a one-track mind; as a matter of fact you haven't demonstrated to me that you even have a half-track brain. Unless you can learn to direct some of those brain cells and misguided energy into THINKING and acting constructively, you will never grow up to be a useful member of society. You have wasted everybody's time with this foolishness and now the ENTIRE class will have to stay after school a half hour so we can finish the lesson." This last edict, although probably outlawed today, was a real killer punishment, for now at least three quarters of the class was mad at you.

Along with what might be considered draconian discipline, we had no show and tell, no art classes, no field trips, no visual aids to speak of (we did have a couple of 16mm documentary movies one year) and, as already noted, no playground equipment or supervised recess. However, just about 100% of us could read well above grade level. We had been exposed to a wide selection of the great literary works of western civilization, were quite familiar with the geography of the world and nation and had a basic knowledge of world and US history. Most important of all, the teachers, and especially Mrs. Morgan, drummed into us the necessity to THINK. She was of the opinion that the average person seldom uses more than a fraction of his or her mental capacity, and she stated many times that her primary goal in teaching was to stimulate her pupils to exceed the average. It was probably a vain hope but, to me, her attitude contains a key to what is often missing in education today.

To a great majority of young people, school has always been a hassle at best and a form of drudgery at worst, and we were certainly no different in that respect. Nevertheless, it is also true that the teachers who drove us harder and were disliked or even hated by many students, were the ones who, we now realize, were the best teachers we had and from whom we learned the most.

Chapter Thirteen

My Dad and President Roosevelt

Maybe it runs in the family or something, but both my Dad and I have had encounters with United States presidents while we were on the water. Not that we were engaged in any protests or other activity that would be likely to get us into trouble. We were merely going about our business when, lo and behold, there was the President alongside on a yacht. I can't predict the future, but many of our presidents have been avid salt-water fishermen, or so it is claimed, and maybe my son will get his shot at it yet; you can never tell.

My Dad's encounter took place during the middle 1930s in the "Race" at the mouth of Long Island Sound. A group of senior vice presidents from the Travelers Insurance Company had chartered the old *ANNA R* to take them fishing and were "Heaving and Hauling" for bluefish with the tarred handlines that most inshore saltwater sportfishing was done with in those days. As a matter of fact, although my Dad was a popular sportfishing guide, he had not yet purchased his first rod and reel. In that era, if you were planning to go fishing on any of the local char-terboats and wanted to use a rod and reel, you had better bring it with you. What you did have to bring, however, was either a pair of heavy gloves (for the sissies) or a new roll of black friction tape (known locally as "Tire Tape") to keep your lily white hands from being cut to ribbons. Taping up your fingers was a necessary part of the ritual every true sportfisherman engaged in on the way out to the fishing grounds. It must have been quite a sight to see six or eight executives, who in the 1920s and 30s commonly went fishing attired in L. L. Bean wool pants and shirt complete with plaid tie, sitting on the deck of an aging, and slightly odifer-ous, lobsterboat trying to tape 2 or 3 fingers on each hand. It was not an easy task to wrap that heavy friction tape on securely enough to keep it from falling off when your hands got wet, but yet loose enough by the joints to allow your fingers to grasp the handline securely. You also could get the tape too tight and cut off the circulation to one or more fingers, especially when you were clumsily struggling to wrap your right-hand fingers with your left hand.

For those of you who are under 40 years of age, I will now take a few paragraphs to explain the heave and haul method of bluefishing. As everyone should have figured out by now, it involved heaving a lure out and hauling it back but, like all simple operations, there was a great deal more to it than first appeared. We will begin with the lure. These came in a great variety of sizes, shapes, and sometimes even colors, but a generic heave and haul jig would be an oval lead and/or block-tin jig about 10 inches long, 1 1/2 inches wide at the base, tapering to about 1/2 inch at the top, and weighing about two pounds. It would normally have a large fixed hook-usually a #1 IP cod hook from Pflueger-at the top end and a 1/4 inch hole for the steel leader at the bottom. If it was an unpainted type, the top half was shined up with a knife blade at regular intervals during the day. In other words, it was the precursor to the diamond jig.

As is done when diamond jigging, the boats were run up-tide (really up the current, but locally called up-tide) until the ranges on the shore were lined up. You then stopped the boat and drifted down-tide towards the rip, meanwhile letting the jig down to the bottom and retrieving it. The heave and haul technique, however, differed in several ways from diamond jigging for, in spite of its being over twice as heavy as a normal chrome-plated diamond jig, the water resistance of over 100 feet of #8 tarred cotton line is greater than 40 lb. mono would be and therefore the heave and haul jig doesn't go to bottom quite as rapidly as the modern diamond jig. This in turn makes it a lot harder to tell when you have reached the bottom, thus increasing the possibility of getting the jig hung-up on the rocks. When that big cod hook got hung-up solidly while you were drifting down-tide at three or four knots, it usually stayed there.

Therefore, in order to tell when the jig had reached bottom, you would let the line run out through your right hand, while you heaved sections of it out with your left, carefully matching the speed at which the lure was sinking. You kept your eyes glued to the line coming off your left hand because, when the lure reached bottom, it would slow slightly and you would throw a loop in the line. You then immediately began to haul the line back with a smooth motion for about 10 or 15 pulls before repeating the procedure.

The proper stance was, as it is in golf, vitally important to success. Standing sideways, feet spread well apart for balance, arms only slightly bent, gripping the line between the thumb and the first two fingers, and keeping your elbows locked, you pulled using the shoulder joints only. You also had to pull quite fast and any jerkiness whatsoever in your motion would probably keep a bluefish from biting the lure. Gripping the line the other way so that the little finger was on the leading side (locally called "Jersey Grabbing" just did not cut the mustard and you could almost hear the bluefish laughing at the erratic motion of the jig.

Lastly, if you had done all the foregoing in a professional manner and had a hook-up, you had to HAUL LIKE HELL, as even a couple inches of slack line would allow the bluefish to throw that fixed hook. This was doubly important when you had the fish near the boat, for if the fish got ahead of you at that point, he could, and very often did, throw that 2 pound jig into the cockpit like a guided missile. Those #1 IP cod hooks, which were almost as large as a small gaff, also had a wicked barb and there were only two ways to remove the hook if it became buried in your anatomy. You could go to the hospital, which naturally spoiled everyone else's day and no he-man worth his salt wanted to do that, or you could take a deep breath and twist the hook the rest of the way through until the point reemerged from the skin. This would allow you to squeeze down the barb with the heavy pliers every boat carried for that purpose, and then the hook could be backed out RELATIVELY easily. This second option was not for the faint-hearted or squeamish and had to be carried out almost immediately before the shock had worn off and you lost your nerve. Needless to say, most corporation vice presidents tended to be nervous about the possibility of being impaled by a errant jig and were consequently not particularly adept at heaving and hauling.

Unfortunately, what most novice fishermen were very good at was getting hung up on the bottom and losing their jigs. This could be the beginning of a bad day for both the angler and the skipper, for if a customer was inattentive and persisted in losing several jigs in a row he might be in line for a bawling out by the captain. Remember, in marked contrast to the 1990s, during the 1930s, most local fishing guides were really lifelong commercial fishermen who today would be described as somewhat lacking in people skills. They had been on the receiving end of many a tirade when they were learning their trade, and most of them were not a bit shy in dishing it out, regardless of the professional standing of the customer in his shoreside job. My Dad, in contrast, was always polite to his customers and had rapidly built a successful business using that approach.

Now that we have got our lesson on the history of inshore sportfishing for bluefish out of the way, let's return to the original subject of my father's encounter with a president. To set the stage, it was a sloppy day with a nasty ebb tide rip and my Dad would start back up the tide (current) before they drifted down to the first breaker. The fish were biting OK, but only on one small section of the rip called the "Tower and Light" spot and any move to either side would produce little in the way of a bluefish. Things were going along fine until an ocean-going yacht over 100 feet long appeared on the scene and began to fish near them. The yacht was on the "grounds" so to speak, but wasn't even close to the right place on the rip (known locally not being within four rows of a... holes of the spot) and, while the gang in my Dad's old lobsterboat was hooking up every drift, the group in the yacht went fishless. Not only that, they were fishing with RODS AND REELS; a fact which gave some of my Dad's customers a good laugh.

Whoever was running the yacht, however, was obviously on the ball because after a couple of unproductive drifts it was plain they had figured out they were not quite in the right place. When my Dad began his next run back up the "tide," the yacht tagged along on his port side, but close aboard. It was the age-old trick of wait until the other boat stops, supposedly in the right place, and then run up ahead of him a short distance and stop. The wind that day was blowing right off the rip at about 25 knots and both boats slowly turned broadside to it after they stopped. Down the tide they drifted and, sure enough, both boats hooked up. My Dad's party using handlines had all landed their bluefish in short order, but the fishermen on the yacht, using RODS AND REELS, were still struggling with their

Dad rigging his FIRST FISHING ROD. A major change from tarred handlines, about 1936.

Dad, aboard ANNA R I, giving fishing advice to customer Lonny Porritt, editor of the Travelers Insurance Co. Magazine, about 1936.

ANNA R I with same fishing party (Porritt) that was aboard during the President Roosevelt encounter, but this photo dates from 1936.

bluefish as both boats drifted ever closer to the breakers in the rip.

As usually occurs when two boats are drifting near each other and one is directly to weather of the other, they tend to close the gap. This had happened to these two and, when my Dad got ready to run back up the drift they were nearly touching. Not only that, by the time he had chugged nearly the length of the 125 foot yacht, he was in the rip broadside and took a couple of waves over the rail. This did not improve his attitude one bit and it began to get worse when he realized that, although he had a head start, the old 8 knot *ANNA R* was going to be caught by that 15 knot yacht before he was half way back to his starting point.

Sure enough, the same thing took place the next drift and, worse still, this time they bucketed a big wave over the port rail and got the whole crew soaking wet. On the way back up the tide to the start of the drift, Lonny Porritt, one of the customers, came up to my Dad and said he had been watching the party on the offending yacht that drift and was almost certain the angler wearing the white shirt and smoking a cigarette in a holder was President Roosevelt. My old man was too annoyed by what was going on to be impressed by this observation and said "I don't care if he's the King of England. He's getting on my nerves and if he pulls that stunt again I'm going to give him a piece of my mind!" Well, he didn't have very long to wait, for the yacht soon caught up to them and proceeded to stop just up the tide from them.

This was just too much for the captain of the *ANNA R* and, as soon as both boats had stopped, he leaned out and shouted "Hey, you on the yacht!" A crewman in what looked to be a navy uniform came to the rail and answered politely "Yes, do you want something?" My Dad was really building up a head of steam by this time and he shot back "Do I want something; you're darn right I want something. What the Hell are you trying to do to me, can't you see that I am trying to make a living here? First you use me for a range because you don't know where the fish are, then you almost drift into me while pushing me down into the rip and getting all of my party wet. Either learn to fish like a civilized man or get that Noah's Ark out of my hair!"

Dead silence on the other boat, while everybody on deck looked, not towards my Dad, but towards the angler smoking a cigarette in a long holder. The President, for it really was he, just sat there for a couple of seconds and then burst into peals of laughter. The others didn't seem to know how to react to either my Dad's outburst or the reaction from the Chief Executive, and most of them just stood there with their mouths gaping open in shock. President Roosevelt waved his free hand in a friendly gesture toward the group on the *ANNA R*, said something to a man in a gold braided hat who was hovering nearby and, in a few moments, the yacht got underway and steamed away to the west until it went over the horizon.

Chapter Fourteen

HOW PRESIDENT EISENHOWER AND I WENT FISHING TOGETHER

I suppose the title is a bit of an overstatement, but what is literary license for, if not to be used now and then? President Eisenhower and I didn't exactly go fishing on the same boat together, but we did fish in close proximity to each other, so maybe it ought to read that the President and I went fishing near each other. However, I like the first title better and it's my story, so that's that.

The encounter took place in the fall of 1958, shortly after my father's bone cancer metastasized from his leg to his spine. His right leg had been amputated above the knee three years earlier in an attempt to arrest the malignancy and it seemed for a while that things were going to be OK. He was able to get back on the boat in a few months and, although he was no longer able to work on deck, he had no trouble running the boat from the flybridge after he managed to hitch his way up the ladder. Once there, he stayed put through thick and thin, hot and cold, wet or dry and would come down only after the charter had gone home.

The old man was tougher than shoe leather when it came to fishing in bad weather. Even after his amputation, I never remember it getting rough enough to drive him down from that exposed bridge. I have seen the seas reach #10 on the Horrendiscope and while I would often become concerned for our safety, he would just grit his teeth and we would POR (press on regardless). By the way, the old Beaufort scale, which has been used by mariners to gauge wind and waves since the middle 1800s, has been supplanted locally by the Horrendiscope scale. This improved method, invented and patented by Captain Thomas McLoughlin, gauges sea conditions relative to the particular vessel one is on and is a much more accurate measure of how deep the do-do is that you have allowed yourself to get into.

At any rate, my father's cancer unfortunately wasn't cured and, even though I knew he wasn't well and was wearing a supportive collar on his neck, he never let on to me that he knew he was going down hill fast. We were headed out to sea one morning when, out of a clear blue sky, he announced that this was going to be the last day he was going to be able to run the boat. I tried to kid him about it and told him it was just another of those bilious attacks he was always complaining about, but he shook his head and said "No, it isn't a bilious attack. The bone cancer has spread to my neck now and that's all there is to it. There's nothing any-body can do about it. I saw Dr. Reynolds last week and he thought I would be able to finish out the season, but my neck is going to pieces a lot faster than the doc-tors thought. I can tell that if we get a rough day, something is going to snap in there and then there will be hell to pay, especially if we have a charter aboard."

As he said, that was all there was to it. He went ashore that night and didn't set foot outside the house again. He never complained to any of us about being struck down at age 62, but it took him a long time to die. Dr. Roger Riley, who mercifully put him on straight morphine when the pain became unmanageable using conventional painkillers, told me his heart was strong enough to last till he was 100. He had a tough life from start to finish, but he made the best of what he had to work with. He and I spent 16 years together on a small boat and what suc-cess I have had on the water primarily derives from his teaching. I just wish I had paid more attention to what he tried to tell me.

To get back to the original subject of the story, I had been thrust abruptly from the cockpit to the flybridge in the space of a few hours. Which is not to say I was unprepared for the job, but we were now in the market for a good permanent deckhand to take my place in the cockpit. This was harder to solve than I antici-pated and, except for weekends and holidays, I did without one for most of three summers. I found out quickly that you can do almost anything when you are 30 years old and healthy. As a matter of fact, you can do just about anything when you are 30 even if you aren't too healthy, as I proved when I managed to fall into an open hatch and break my foot about two weeks after I took over the boat. The doctor wanted to put me in a cast, but I persuaded him to fabricate a steel plate shaped to the bottom of my sole so I could bind my foot to it with an Ace ban-dage. This enabled me to wear a boot so I could work on deck. I also had to bor-row a crutch, as my foot was much too painful the first week to do anything but stand gingerly on it. Between the crutch and hopping around on one leg, I found I could manage just fine, although hopping any distance while wearing over-knee boots got to be rather tiring.

So, there we were that fine September morning at Block Island North Rip, trolling for bluefish and green bonita. The tide was flooding and we were fishing down-tide of the rip, about half way from the end of the point to #1 BI buoy. It had taken me nearly an hour of searching, but I had finally located a school of fish lying just off the bottom parallel to the edge of the bank. I took a quick range on the spot (this was before lorans) and, by making long tows, we were hooking one or two fish each way. In addition to having trouble locating the fish, part of my problem that morning was that the species of bait the fish were feeding on had changed from what it had been previously and we were using the wrong lure. The day before, they had been biting well on the tried and true Royal Gismo tube lures so I naturally started out using them, but without much success. I then switched to #15 Tony Acetta Pet spoons, with a two ounce weight between the 25 foot mono leader and the monel wire line to keep the spoons from wandering all over the place and tangling together. This was a big improvement and we settled down to what is called a "steady pick".

We had *picked* about two dozen mixed blues and bonita and things were going along smoothly with only an occasional tangle, when I noticed a couple of fairly large yachts headed toward us from the direction of Newport. One of them appeared to be a converted PT boat and the other was an odd looking vessel that had the hull of a Trumpy, but with double spreader outriggers and a couple of regular Rockaway fishing chairs bolted to the aft deck. The PT boat was painted flat black, and the yacht, which was originally white, had yellowed along the waterline above the fine crop of grass which showed every time she lifted in the swell. All told, a rather motley pair.

The ominous looking black PT boat was holding station abeam of the white yacht and you didn't have to be Sherlock Holmes to figure out that something out of the ordinary was going on. I was talking on the marine radio with Joe Chaptelaine from Pt. Judith who was fishing down at Southeast Light and I mentioned the "Odd Couple" who had begun to drag some lines about a quarter of a mile away. Chappy came right back with an answer. "I'll bet that's President Eisenhower. He's supposed to be in Newport for a meeting this week. Take a peek at them with the binoculars if they get close enough and let me know if I'm right." I agreed it certainly looked like the black PT boat was riding shotgun for the white one. Perhaps it was the President after all.

While it was certainly interesting that it was probably President Eisenhower over there, I was more concerned they would come over to where I was trolling and screw up my pass. It was difficult enough to keep the *ANNA R* right on the edge of the drop-off while towing across the current, without having some novice try to cross us at right angles and demand the right of way. The two boats kept edging closer and, sure enough, there was Ike in the port chair hanging onto a rod with what had to be over a hundred yards of monofilament stretched behind the yacht. I told the charter what was going on, and they were all a-twitter about the situation. I didn't say much, but I was thinking to myself "Shoot, I hope they don't decide to cross ahead of us, I don't think the President will be very thrilled if I accidentally cut his lure off. On the other hand, it will probably be the only strike he's going to get today unless one of the fish commits suicide."

Whoever was running the yacht might not have known how to troll for bluefish, but he was a good boat-handler and a gentleman. By the time he had worked his way down to where we were running in and out, I'm sure he could plainly see we were catching fish each pass, but he never tried to interfere with me in the slightest. People on all three of the boats were, by then, watching each other with the binoculars, the *ANNA R's* passengers to look at the President and the other two trying to see what we were doing that they were not. After a bit, the two of them began to run parallel to my course with the black boat in between the white yacht and the *ANNA R*. This was worse than useless. When they were going in one direction, the white yacht would be in 75 feet of water, well off the bank, and when headed in the opposite direction they would be in only 12 feet, almost on top of the bar. The situation was beginning to be a little embarrassing to me, for unlike most novices, they were so polite my conscience was beginning to bother me, especially as I was a fan of the President and wanted badly for him to catch something. It's always pleasing to show you have superior skills at something, but my Dad had taught me that you have no right to rub it in. I was mulling this over in my mind as I was hopping around the cockpit on one leg unhooking fish, setting lines and steering with the tiller. I don't know how busy a one-armed paperhanger is, but he would have had competition from me that fall and I had little patience for distracting influences.

Normally the chatter on my marine radio was not a bother, but since our visitors had arrived there had been a lot of interference, caused, I found out later, by spill-over from whatever super-secret channels the two yachts were using to communicate with each other. It soon got on my nerves and I turned the darn thing off to get rid of the static. Shortly after I did that, the customer who currently had possession of the binoculars told me that someone on the secret-service boat was making motions as if he wanted to contact me on the radio. I didn't have time to fool around trying to find their channel, so I waved for him to come alongside. The operator of the PT was a damn good boat driver; he goosed her up a bit, swung up on my starboard side about 10 feet away and steadied her up. I'll admit I regretted waving him over when that big ark was rumbling up on me, but he held her there, straight as an arrow.

One of the burly young men standing on the deck came to the rail and said "The gentleman over on the white yacht would like to know what lure you are using." I explained the combination of #15 Pet spoon and weight and offered to give him one to bring over to the other boat. He thanked me politely, but said it would not be necessary as they had told him they had all types of lures over there. They just wanted to know specifically what lure it was. With that, they swung off and resumed station about 150 feet from my beam. You could see them talking back and forth on the radios and a flurry of activity going on over on the President's yacht. However, they were still dragging at least a hundred yards of mono behind them, so it was a sure bet they were still digging through their tackle boxes looking for spoons. Meanwhile we were going back and forth on about a half mile run and catching at least two fish each way.

This exercise went on for another pass with no effort on their part to change any lures and you just knew that they didn't have any spoons. Sure enough, there came the PT boat alongside again, sheepishly asking to buy some tackle from me. I replied that I didn't have any tackle for sale, but I would be glad to give them a couple of rigs and they could give them to the President with my compliments. This time we had to get close enough for one of my customers to pass the gear across from hand to hand as I couldn't leave the tiller for long or the boats might swing together. I could turn out of his way easily, but he couldn't turn that 90 footer quickly enough to avoid me if I took a sudden sheer. I'll just say that we pulled it off without a hitch.

It was becoming plain by this time that Ike was getting disturbed by their inability to get a single bite, especially as we were now hauling them in every few minutes. I also knew from reading about his war-time career as Supreme Allied Commander that he was reputed to have a very short fuse when it came to inefficiency. I was thinking I wouldn't want to be the captain on the white yacht about now, when I saw the black PT with the secret service men coming over to hail me again. He swung alongside and the same guy came to the rail and said "The fellow on the white yacht would like to have you come over and talk to him if you can stop fishing for a minute. He says that he has some questions to ask and he doesn't want to filter the information through any lieutenants." There was really no question about what our answer was going to be. After all, it was almost a command performance and was definitely an offer that nobody in his right mind would turn down.

We smoked those lines in at a record pace and made ready to meet the President of the United States. I told the charter to make sure that none of them were foolish enough to reach into a pocket for something while we were there or there would probably be a large hole in their forehead before they could blink an eye. Those secret service men were all smiling affably, but it wouldn't be a good idea to have one of them think you were reaching for a weapon, no sir.

The President's yacht had pulled up their port outrigger when we approached and, as we closed with them, it was quite plain that Ike was PISSED. I was now thoroughly convinced I didn't want to be aboard the yacht with them. There was not a happy camper in the bunch and the most unhappy camper of them all was the Chief Executive. He was sitting sort of slouched down in the Rockaway fighting chair with, of all things, a GOLF hat on his head. I had this wild impulse to holler over and tell him it was no wonder he wasn't getting any bites with that GOLF hat on his head but, on the other hand, I didn't want my wife to have to raise the kids all alone, so I kept my mouth shut.

Ike stood up and it was plain that it was going to be his turn to speak. He didn't speak, he roared. There was really no need for me to come alongside, you could have heard him a half a mile away in the engine room of a 6/71 powered lobster-boat running wide open. "What the Hell are these dumb bastards doing wrong? We've been watching you haul them in, one after the other, for over an hour, and we haven't had a nibble. I know the Goddamn navy doesn't know beans about fishing, but this is ridiculous. The friggin Secret Service won't let me go on a boat that they haven't checked out, but I've got half a mind to jump over there right now and to hell with them!" Whew, he sure hadn't needed any speech-writer to draft that one up. I was really tickled by the outburst; there was a man after my own heart, a soldier's soldier who you could and would follow into any battle. Here he was, the President of the United States of America and he was reacting exactly as I would have if I was getting my ass kicked on the fishing grounds.

It was apparently my turn now, for Ike was obviously waiting for some pearls of wisdom from me, and they had better be good. The funny thing about "my turn" is that, although Ike's words are still burned into my brain over 35 years later, I really can't remember much of what I said to him. I guess my brain was in a time warp of some sort after the President had finished delivering his address. My mind was so filled with admiration for the man that everything I said and did after he spoke is foggy. The party said afterwards I calmly explained that the fish were concentrated in a narrow strip and, if they would line-up right behind me when I made the next run, I would lead them over the spot. The President thanked me for the advice, and he must have ordered the boat operator to do as

I suggested for, in the middle of their first pass, they finally managed to hook a bonita and land it. We all cheered when they got it in the boat and Ike gave his famous clenched hands over the head move, but this time it was for our benefit and not for the press. I guess all Ike wanted was to succeed at catching a fish because, when I got ready to lead them down the next run they waved good-by and took off towards Newport.

My wife usually listened to the short wave receiver during the afternoon in order to hear the charterboats batting the breeze on their way home. This gave her a rough idea as to what we had done (unless we were lying about it) and when we expected to get in. It also gave us the chance to send messages and instructions home. It was a good deal, she could listen but she couldn't reply, which was OK with me most of the time. From her standpoint, I'm sure many days she probably was beating the devil out of the radio in frustration from not being able to talk back. At any rate, while I was certainly pleased with meeting the President and tried to fill her in by telling the other boats what had gone on, I didn't make a big deal out of it. You can imagine my surprise when we arrived at the dock and found several photographers and reporters on hand, ready to tell the world how the home town boy had made good.

The story made a pretty big splash in the local papers and the following night I got a call from a reporter who said he was from the New York Times. This was really the big-time, but it was a one shot affair and, because I never heard from Time Magazine or Newsweek, I figured it was all over. My one moment of fleeting glory and then kerplunk, back to obscurity. Little did I know what usually happens to people who are thrown into contact with a President and make the New York Times. I can never be fully convinced it was just a coincidence that a scant month after the meeting, I had a notice from the IRS that they wanted to conduct a full scale audit, and I should appear in their offices and bring all my records. You would have to still believe in the tooth fairy to swallow their line that it was a random selection; random, my foot!

The Sept. 4, 1958, New London Day picture of me showing type of fishing lures I gave to President Eisenhower.

Chapter Fifteen

THE HARINGS

Of all the characters my brother and I associated with during our "Growing Up" period, the Harings, Alfred and Cornelia, were definitely the most unforgettable and I thought it only fitting that I write something about them that will serve to recognize that, they too, had a definite impact on our family. Al and Neil, for that was what they preferred to be called, came into our life in about 1936 or 1937 when they bought Louie Olson's waterfront house and rowboat rental business. For those who are either young or newcomers to Noank, the Olson house sat on what is now an overgrown lot at the foot of Snake Hill (where Palmer Court becomes Riverview Avenue) and was a 2 1/2 story building painted a rather nondescript shade of green. Unlike most Noank homes, it sat on a cement slab and the lower floor served as a basement and storage room, with the actual entrance to the living quarters being through the presently weed-choked gate part way up the hill. The distance from the house to the shoreline was probably less than 75 feet and, while there was some scraggly grass here and there, the main use of their front lawn was a parking lot for their rowboat rental customers.

Reaching out from the seawall at the outer edge of the parking area was a long, ramshackle dock, complete with several roughly built storage sheds perched precariously on the decking. One of these sheds was an outhouse or privy which, in time honored Noank custom, discharged its products directly into the sea. On the north side of the dock some of the rental rowboats were tied-off to a series of metal and wooden stakes, with the southwest side of the dock being used for larger boats and Al Haring's 24 foot lobsterboat *ADA MAY*. The remainder of their fleet of rowboats was tied bow-to-stern in groups of 2 or 3 and secured to moorings situated along the inner edge of the flats across the channel, with the *ADA MAY* primarily used as a towboat to ferry them back and forth as needed. As far as the house itself, I was only inside once while it was still owned by the Olson's and all I can remember about the place was that they had a 6-foot stuffed polar bear standing upright in the living room.

By any measure, the Harings were an unusual pair to be embarking on the rental rowboat business. Al had been raised in Norwich and was a burly, soft spoken man who never appeared to loose his cool or raise his voice beyond a conversational level. It was said by some, that even at his marriage when he was asked the usual question, he replied, "Well, I suppose so," rather than the conventional "I do". Neil, on the other hand, was forceful, politely plain-spoken and, when riled, had a vocabulary of profanity that would have startled the toughest construction worker. As a matter of fact, Neil's penchant for bellowing graphic expletives when she was really ticked-off, such as when a transient yacht speeded by her fuel dock, gained her a measure of fame along the waterfront for, when Neil was at full volume, she could be plainly understood at least a half mile away. This unlady-like behavior was in marked contrast to Noank's accepted social conduct for females of that era and, in retrospect, I believe it may have been one of the reasons the Harings never became a true part of Noank's community life.

Interestingly, this unusual couple with almost totally divergent personalities were both were very well educated people. Al had a masters degree in geology from Columbia and Neil had a bachelors degree in animal husbandry from Rutgers and was certified as a milk tester in the state of New Jersey.

Although we were not aware of it for years and they certainly never gave any indication of it as far as their lifestyle in Noank was concerned, Neil was independently wealthy. We knew they wintered in East Orange, New Jersey at a house she had inherited from her father but, until I was nearly an adult, we were unaware of the extent of her finances. My brother John and I were invited down to visit them several times, and we were really impressed, to say the very least. The house was a three story brick semi-mansion of about 15 rooms, plus 4 or 5 baths, and had speaking tubes in all the upper floors running down to what were once the servants' quarters and kitchen. The place was pretty much unchanged from its Victorian configuration, with a game room on the third floor housing a full size billiard table surrounded with glass cases holding a massive collection of stuffed game birds, nests and, of course, eggs. The only recent remodeling was on the servants' level where Al, who was an avid photographer, had converted one of the rooms into a lavishly equipped darkroom.

Neil's father, Mr. Hussey, had been in the wholesale plumbing business, which really showed in the bathrooms, for it was the only time I have seen a shower with 5 shower heads. It further turned out that her family still owned an entire block in downtown Manhattan between 41st and 42nd Street, running from 9th to 10th Avenue. Not only that, her grandfather had owned the land on which R.H. Macy built his store and had given Mr. Macy what I believe was a 99-year lease on the property instead of selling it to him. While the yearly payments to the Husseys turned out to be peanuts when inflation was factored in, the lease eventually turned into a real bonanza sometime in the 1950s when Macy somehow let it lapse for a year and a day and Neil's brother, Fred, threatened them with eviction.

At the time when the Harings first became our neighbors, my brother and I, at 7 and 9 years of age, were what might have been described as wharf rats. We sort of adopted the Harings as an extra aunt and uncle. Almost every summer day we would trudge over and hang around in the hope we would be allowed to help by bailing out the rowboats and other assorted chores. Unfortunately this diversion was shattered by the 1938 hurricane which destroyed all but three of their rowboat fleet, piled the shattered pieces of the dock in the middle of the road and washed half the underpinning of the house away. For the rest of that fall, John and I were too occupied by our own family's problems to pay much attention to what the Harings were doing but, sometime before spring, Al had the rest of the house torn down. Even now, I am baffled by Al's motives in tearing down a readily fixable house (the living quarters were only superficially damaged) but I guess he couldn't face up to living through another hurricane that close to the water. After the house was removed, Al had a small storage shed built on the site and they attempted to operate the rental rowboat business out of it for the 1939 season. This proved to be a major hassle for them and their customers, for they had not been able to rebuild the dock. This, in turn, forced them to land and launch the rowboats from the beach and seriously limited the operation. Sometime during 1939, they bought the Freeman Rodgers/Parker Wildes boatyard, where Orion Ford now has his lobster business, and moved their operation up there during the winter.

Although their new property included the lot on the west side of Riverview Avenue on which there was an old run-down house formerly occupied by Parker Wildes and his family (now the middle of Pat Fritzsche's front lawn) Al considered the house not fit for habitation and it just stood there unoccupied and deteriorating for many years. The damaged 2-story building fronting on the southeast side of Riverview Avenue had, at an earlier time, housed a paint store on the main floor and an apartment on the second, which had once been the home of my somewhat eccentric school-mate Emory Sherman. Al had the top floor torn off and a roof built over the defunct paint store. An apartment, of sorts, was installed on the main floor, consisting of a single room with a heavy curtain separating the eating and sleeping section in the rear from what, with charity, could be thought of as a narrow sitting room in the front. All this took place long before Noank had a public water system and as Neil had a phobia against cisterns (she considered them horribly unsanitary) water was piped into the apartment via a 3/4 inch galvanized steel pipe running under the road to an old well adjacent to the vacant house. The apartment Al built would have been minimum accommodations for a working couple just starting out in life but, surprisingly, the Harings put up with it for over 10 years until they bought a nice home at the top of New London Road in Mystic.

The years 1940 and 1941 saw a flurry of activity at the former boatyard. The first step was to remove the huge piles of wreckage and remains of several boats from the shoreline. Al then contracted with one of the Maxons in West Mystic to provide a new fleet of rowboats; docks were built to replace those destroyed in the hurricane; several small buildings were put up adjacent to the water; and a Mr. Richmond from somewhere in Rhode Island erected what was always referred to as the "Tin Shed". The Harings next had the Gulf Oil Corporation install gasoline pumps on the dock, Al opened a combination bait shop and snack bar in one of the new buildings on the waterfront and my brother and I graduated to cleaning boats in exchange for soda pop and candy bars. Things were really looking up for the Harings, but the increased activity in their new location was short lived, for the declaration of war on December 8, 1941 signaled the virtual cessation of pleasure boating activity for the duration, so Al, who was an avowed pacifist and would have made a dreadful soldier anyway, took a job as a chipper on the night shift at Electric Boat.

Even though neither of them complained to any of us about their situation, the war years imposed a number of definite drawbacks for the Harings. For one thing, it meant they could no longer spend their winters in her very comfortable New Jersey residence, but had to live year round in a drafty, uninsulated summer cottage with only a couple of kerosene space heaters to fight the cold. Secondly, the Harings were not only very private people who, as far as I know, didn't belong to any religious, fraternal or service organizations, but also didn't fit in socially on the local level. To the best of my knowledge, other than my family and some casual acquaintances among their customers, they had no adult acquaintances who could be considered close friends. In our family, my Dad was working days as an electrician at Electric Boat, with time off every fall to serve as one of the three Town of Groton assessors, and my Mom was working part time at the Town Hall. As for the Harings, Al was chipping welds on the night shift at EB six days out of seven, with the result that Neil was home alone nearly every night for the duration of the war.

My Mom was sympathetic to Neil's situation and as long as we kept up our grades and had finished our homework on time, my brother and I were often allowed to go up after supper and spend a few hours visiting and playing cards or Monopoly with Neil. Besides that, our family was into the classics, musically, and often my Dad settled down to an evening of the London Philharmonic. This normally bored John and me to tears and we would dash through our homework so we could go up to see Neil, for she had a good collection of "pop" records which were more to our liking. At her place there were no London Philharmonic concertos, we were treated to Benny Goodman, Glenn Miller, Jo Stafford, Harry James, Jinny Simms and other recording artists. Above all else, Neil was a big fan of Dinah Shore and bought every one of her 78s as soon as they were released. She also had some of the first Calypso records we had heard and I can still remember parts of *The Gitchee and the Monkey* and *Hot Dog, Hot Doggie* after nearly 50 years.

There was one minor drawback to the visits, namely the presence of their English Mastiff which Al, who raised him from a pup, had named "Opie". Opie was now full grown, which means he was between large and huge, and like most English Mastiffs, was a world class drooler. While Opie was a reasonably friendly 150 pound dog (although the Harings always fitted him with a strong steel choker collar just in case), he was subject to chronic ear infections that made him rather testy at times, to say the least. Also, he was perpetually hungry and, even after wolfing down 5 or 6 pounds of dog food, was inclined to beg unashamedly when Neil served us light refreshments such as cake or ice cream. A persistent 150 pound dog can be rather hard to ignore and, as Opie just loved sweets, you had to keep your eyes on him every minute or he would clean off your plate in a heartbeat.

It was actually a bit unnerving to be in the same room with him because when you were sitting down and Opie was ambling around the waxed linoleum floor on all four gangly legs, the two of you were on the same eye level. He would stand there in front of you gazing sorrowfully at your dessert with his rheumy eyes, drool hanging down in long strings from each side of his jaw and slowly dripping on the floor, when the bothersome infection in his ears would slowly overcome his

Neil Haring, John Rathbun and me, at about 17 years, on stoop of Haring's office.

Al Haring, 1946.

salivating reflex and his head would give a tiny twitch. This was the clue we all learned to keep an eye out for, as it was followed in about 2 seconds by Opie vigorously shaking his head. It was then *Watch Out Folks* for anyone within 6 feet, especially if you happened to be seated alongside him when he began. The first snap of his massive head would shoot the sticky drool out like liquid projectiles in an arc ranging from floor to ceiling and all points in between. He usually got off about 10 to 15 shakes in an increasing crescendo of flailing ears and loosely flapping jowls which emitted showers of sticky spittle. Furthermore, if you think the deluge of canine saliva was the only hazard we contended with in those situations, you would be mistaken, for it was accompanied by his loudly clanking collar, as the heavy steel ring on the loose end of the choker chain smashed back and forth with the speed of light. Even Neil, who backed down from no one, kept out of the way when Opie was in the throes of a full scale drool explosion. As soon as Opie shuddered to a stop, everyone would get a square or two of toilet paper and go around wiping the goo from the walls, floor and furniture. A few times, we missed a glob that had landed on one of the playing cards and didn't discover it until we tried to shuffle the deck, only to find two of the cards stuck together in a rather disgusting manner. Al and Neil may have loved that dog, but if it had been up to me, Opie would never have seen another sunrise.

The post-war years from 1945 to 1953 were busy times at the Haring rowboat livery, with a big demand for small boat fishing, a minimal supply of small private boats available and plenty of fish close to shore. In our area, the current proliferation of marinas was not even envisioned and there were only a few places catering to the entry-level boater. Although there were a scattering of minor players such as Mitchell on Masons Island and what later became Freddy's Boat Livery in Stonington, the local small boat rental market was dominated by Harry Shaffer on Masons Island, the Spicers in Groton and the Harings in Noank. The ADA MAY had been a casualty of the 1938 hurricane and Al, who seldom bought only one of anything, especially when it came to hand tools, had Maxon build him two short, extra beamy skiffs for towboats. One, designated number 12, was about 11 feet long and was, as best as I can remember, about 5 feet wide. Number 12 was ordinarily not used as a rental until all the remaining boats were taken and, even then, was usually restricted to two people who Neil would emphatically order to stay in the harbor or suffer the dire consequences of her extreme displeasure when they returned. The second tug designated as "H" and only about 10 feet long, was bought for a spare and never left the tin shed until it was sold by Neil when she went out of the rowboat rental business.

In 1954 Hurricane Carol caused a third major set-back to the Haring's operation. Although hurricane warnings had been posted the day before, the storm was still south of Cape Hatteras and only moving north at 10 miles per hour. Like many local boatman, Al figured he had all the next day to get prepared in the unlikely event it was going to come ashore here. Fortunately for the Rathbun operation, we had been bluefishing in the Race the day before the storm hit. It was raining steadily and blowing about 30 knots from the east, and by noon there was a big swell rolling through from the south-east. When the tide turned ebb it built

Neil Haring working on their rental boats, 1946.

up a savage rip and soon it became really unsafe to get anywhere near the break-ers. As happens in the Race during really heavy weather, every once in awhile, the swell and the waves in the rip would become synchronized and a 12 foot comber would come charging out of the first line of breakers at about 15 knots and race up ahead for at least 500 feet. My Dad considered the unusually heavy swell to be a clear sign that the weather bureau had screwed up again and we were in for it. He wrapped up the trip early even though the fish were biting furiously and we hot-footed it for Noank at our usual top speed of 8 knots. As soon as the charter was unloaded, we gathered up some fenders and extra lines, took the boat to Mystic and tied it securely to Cottrell's dock.

The 8 P.M. weather report still claimed that hurricane Carol was churning around a little below Cape Hatteras with a forward motion of about 10 miles per hour on a northerly course and indicated we would have nothing to be seriously concerned about for at least 24 hours. My Dad was not at all impressed by this forecast. Citing the fact that we already had a low pressure area over us and an unusually heavy swell in the Race, he made several uncomplimentary remarks about the Weather Bureau's overly complacent attitude. Sure enough, by day-break the next morning, it was blowing nearly 50 knots and the radio was issuing a frantic hurricane warning. During the night, the forward motion of Carol had increased to 45 miles per hour and the full fury of the hurricane was now pre-dicted to strike Long Island, and us, by midmorning. My Dad took off for Mystic to stay with the boat and I was delegated to take care of the home front.

Before the day was over, Hurricane Carol had dealt the Noank area a hard blow which was second only to the 1938 hurricane in respect to wind velocity and high water, but thankfully, caused only a fraction of the damage to the village. At the height of the storm the road in front of our house was under 18 inches of water and the waves were striking the south side of my house and shooting up almost to the bottom of the second floor windows. Part of our dock was swept away and

John Rathbun and Al Haring in front of Haring's tackle store, 1946.

we had 2 feet of salt water in the basement when the high water poured down the cellar way. Unfortunately, the Harings really took a licking for they were almost totally unprepared. Their truck was smashed up; about a third of their docks were destroyed; the tackle shop building was washed up into the middle of the parking lot; and over half their rowboats were reduced to kindling wood.

This was the beginning of the end for their rental rowboat business, which was not the unmitigated disaster it might seem, for times were changing; fiberglass boats were coming into their own and America's boating boom was getting underway. The Harings adapted quickly to these developments and Al began to rent more space to private boatmen while concentrating on the tackle store. Neil then took over the job of working the fuel dock and turned it into a major share of their revenue. Things were looking up again for the Haring's enterprise until a personal tragedy intervened. Al, whose skin had always been prone to moles, disregarded a large one on his shoulder that had changed color and begun to grow. It soon developed into a malignant melanoma and, although he had it removed surgically that winter, the cancer had spread throughout his body. By the middle of the next summer, he was no longer able to work and died a few months later.

The next spring, Neil asked us if we would like to take over the tackle shop and have Rosalie help her run the fuel dock. This turned into a full-time summer operation for both Rosalie and several of my teen-age children. I dragged the tackle store building up from the waterfront using rollers and a come-along and attached it to the back of the building where Orion Ford now has his lobster pound. We next converted the combined buildings into a tackle store, expanded the store's line of merchandise by two-fold and, within a year, had quadrupled the gross sales. Rosalie and Neil made a good team on the dock and, by working together, managed to double the amount of fuel pumped. Rosalie would open the dock and tackle shop at the crack of dawn to catch the early morning fishermen and Neil, who never came in before 9 A.M., would stay until dark to get the late evening stragglers. The two of them would be on duty in the middle of the day for the yacht trade, while one of our kids would man the tackle shop, so the whole set-up worked out well for all of us.

My wife Rosalie on Haring's fuel dock, 1970s.
Photographer: Al Haring.

Neil and Rosalie soon developed a great relationship and the two women made an almost unforgettable team. Most of the time, both of them would be dressed in blue coveralls with Gulf Oil Company logos and, to the transient boaters, looked like a mother and daughter pair of local characters. Even when she was not sporting the Gulf Oil Company colors, Neil always dressed rather mannishly, with blue jeans, a man's shirt and black work shoes her usual everyday garb. As a matter of fact, although I had been a guest in their New Jersey home and therefore had seen Neil dressed up to go out to a fine restaurant, the only other time I remember seeing her in a skirt and high heels was at Al's funeral. Her choice of clothing, plus her outspoken mannerisms and truly creative cursing often gave the erroneous impression to strangers that she was uneducated and not very feminine. Nothing could have been further from the truth. She was a true feminist before it had become fashionable to be one and was ahead of her time as far as the female dress code was concerned. In today's world, hardly anyone would give either her attitudes, her "colorful" language or her clothing a second thought.

The two women worked together for about five years and both the fuel gallonage on Neil's dock and our tackle store gross sales maintained a slow but steady growth. Sadly, all good things eventually come to an end and one did not have to be a doctor to know that Neil was developing some sort of a health problem. She began to loose weight and was coming in later and later in the morning. Neil had always been a heavy smoker of Lucky Strikes and we just figured the cigarettes were beginning to get to her, especially as she never gave any other indication that she was not well. The first real sign that she might be seriously ill came when she shut the dock down for the winter and told us it was doubtful if she was going to open up the next spring. We had known her for nearly 30 years but, when asked for a reason, her lifelong reticence concerning details about her private life became very evident. She made it quite plain to us that any more discussion on the subject was totally unwelcome. There was no use in pursuing the subject any further and, after a few unsuccessful attempts to reach her by phone, we lost contact with her that winter.

Actually, this was not unusual, for she was often away during the winter months and the fact that nobody was at home on New London Road was more the rule than the exception. All of a sudden, we saw a short obituary in the New London Day giving notice of her demise, but with no information about details. True to the last in her resolve to keep control of her privacy, she had not only hidden from us the fact she was suffering from inoperable breast cancer, but had made certain her funeral arrangements would not be public. We found out afterwards that she had spent her last days with Orion Ford and Minnie Hart here in Noank. Her brother's family settled her estate and what became of Al's collection of over 50 antique guns, his numerous Leica cameras, tens of thousands of black and white photographs and a workshop full of duplicate tools was never revealed to us.

All told, it was a somewhat unsatisfactory climax to a fairly close personal relationship spanning over 30 years, in which I had grown from a 9-year old wharf rat to a relatively successful fisherman. My wife, Rosalie, and I had been both friends, employees and lessees of the Harings and had always understood that, while we were without doubt the closest friends they had in Noank, there was also an undefinable space between us, which they always chose to maintain. Whatever the reason for their decision to distance themselves from being an integral factor in Noank's community life, they were two of the nicest and most unforgettable characters I have ever known and I will be forever thankful for the privilege of knowing them.

Chapter Sixteen

AFTER HIGH SCHOOL, WHAT DO YOU DO THEN?

Like many people who have reached what some misguided idiot has characterized as the "Golden Years", I've found myself becoming increasingly introspective. During the course of these sometimes troublesome excursions into self-analysis, I have very often viewed what I ended up doing for a living with mixed emotions. However, on balance, it was probably as good a choice for me as any and might even have been the result of a genetic flaw programmed into me at conception. The reason I mention this possibility comes from an amateurish foray into genealogical research I conducted a few years ago, whereby I stumbled on a startling fact. Ever since my heterodox Anabaptist ancestors were ejected by the Puritans from the Massachusetts Colony and settled Block Island in 1662, all my direct male line were employed in some sort of maritime activity. With this inherited proclivity for working at sea hard-wired into my psyche, I was probably unable to countermand my built-in "Marching Orders" by choosing a land-based occupation. I do know, from childhood on, making a living from the sea was my primary goal in life and, even during high school, there was absolutely no question in my mind concerning the choice. This despite my high school guidance teacher's desperate attempts to persuade me to, "Get a college education so you can make something of yourself," as she rather bluntly put it.

In the conventional sense, I suppose she was absolutely correct in trying to steer me toward college. Figuratively speaking though, you can't be what and where you are without first having been what and where you were (think that one over for a minute) and I'm reasonably satisfied with what I've been able to accomplish up to now. I guess the main reason for my eventual contentment with how things worked out is based on the fact that my choice of career, if in fact the fates ever actually offered me a choice, allowed me to participate in the "Last Hurrah" for open-access commercial fishing in America. If you look at the big picture, I think it's safe to say there is an ongoing worldwide evolution in the way fisheries managers think about harvesting protein from the sea. Intellectually, I am fully aware that the rapidly increasing number of restrictions facing today's commercial fishermen are considered by most managers to be absolutely necessary to protect a public resource from our own abuses. At the same time, it's emotionally disturbing for me to realize that none of my descendants will ever have the same opportunity as I had to participate in the fishery where, when and how I chose.

If you stop and think about it, my generation was part of a transition in American family life. We were only the second generation in the entire history of the human race to have what we today consider a *normal* childhood, in that the vast majority of youths were not forced to go to work in order to assist their parents in putting enough food on the table. Although human groupings have always had a privileged class who were spared the necessity of child labor to help their family survive, be it on the farm, at sea or in the sweatshops, the generations which grew up in the U.S.A. from the 1900s onward were the first ones in which almost all children had a fair chance for a high school education and the spare time activities most so-called *Experts* now consider a requirement for balanced growth. As a case in point, my forebears were typical of the preceding generations when great grandfather Bill Gadd Rathbun went to sea before he was 11 and my maternal grandfather left Denmark for America when he was 12 to escape the horrible conditions at the factory where his stepmother had sent him to work. Don't forget, Nathaniel Palmer was already on his third sealing voyage and had been promoted to captain of the sloop HERO when he discovered Antarctica in 1820 at the ripe old age of 21.

From my standpoint, I could hardly wait to finish my senior year at Fitch High School for it would have a two-fold benefit. Getting my diploma would finally get my mother off my back-she was adamant that I graduate-and she would then allow me to get on with the business of commercial fishing. I guess I must have been a real pain in the neck that winter, both to her and especially to the teachers who were urging me to attend college. I had come to the conclusion (well before Robert Fulgum's book made the notion fashionable) that I had learned almost everything of value that would be necessary for a productive life in Grammar School and I was now just going through the motions and wasting everyone's valuable time. This is not to put down the value of a high school education, but I think there is a lot of room for curriculum improvement which would benefit the ability of the AVERAGE student to function well when he or she gets out in the real world. For instance, I had already learned basic math in Grammar School and it has turned out to be very valuable. However, I have never needed to use the trigonometry and solid geometry I took in high school. A course in personal finance would have been more to the point for anyone not planning to be an engineer. Education aside, by working as a deckhand on my Dad's boat that spring I had pushed my unexcused absences to the brink of truancy action by the school. It was therefore a big relief for all concerned when graduation day finally arrived and, to the accompaniment of the school band's rendition of Pomp and Circumstance, I was finally freed for whatever the sea had in store for me.

The first order of business was naturally employment on the family boat for the reminder of the summer but, beyond that, my options for the late fall and winter were open. At the time I graduated in 1946, my Dad's fishing charter business had not yet recovered from the enforced shut-down imposed during WW-2 and we were primarily lobstering. However, the combination of the two fisheries kept us busy until the first of October when my Dad had to go to his winter job in the Groton Assessor's office. I was then faced with a rather dim prospect, for in marked contrast to present conditions, the bluefish had been virtually absent from the Race since 1941 and small fish had only begun to trickle back to their old fishing grounds in late August 1944. By 1946, they were still not present in large numbers and only averaged about a pound and a half dressed weight. They also conformed to the pattern of most coastal migratory species whose stocks are low by arriving late and leaving early. The old New England fisherman's adage "The earlier they come, the later they leave" is true in reverse as well, and, for the first few years after their return, the bluefish began to leave the Race shortly after Labor Day.

With the bluefish option unavailable, I spent most of October handlining for blackfish in the Race, alone. However, while I was catching between 100 to 200 lbs. a day on the days I could get out, at a price of 5 cents per pound at the dock, I barely broke even after fuel and bait expenses were deducted, to say nothing of making a profit. In the meantime, I had noticed Ned Rostron poking around in a mysterious manner on the flats every morning and, after some sleuthing, discovered he was doing very well dredging for bay scallops. I figured if he was making a good dollar right in front of my house, I probably ought to give bay scalloping a whirl so I rigged up a hand dredge, borrowed the family skiff and went in the scallop business.

The skiff was actually a 10-foot rowboat (locally called a Sharpie) built for my Dad by Elmer Davis to replace the one destroyed by the 1938 hurricane and was quite small for the job when loaded down with 5 bushels of scallops and my gear. Being only 18 years old at the time, I gave little thought to the fact it was a truly minimal operation. While I didn't yet own an outboard motor, the beds were only a couple hundred yards from our dock. I got along fairly well by rowing until a gang of experienced scallopers from Saybrook arrived with their big outboard-powered skiffs and glass-bottomed spotters. This was my first contact with real pros, and I suddenly found out I wasn't nearly as smart as I had thought. As a matter of fact, I was at a serious disadvantage for their spotters were much more efficient than dredging in the heavy eelgrass beds, and their vastly superior mobility enabled them to make two drifts to my one, especially if it was blowing hard. I got the message and quickly fabricated a spotter, but stubbornly stuck to my rowing even when the scallops on the flats in front of Noank played out and we had to move up the river to some grounds around Abigail's Island and off Willow Point.

The extra distance required a good half hour row each way in calm weather but, once I got there, the area was fairly small and, as long as the water was clear enough to see bottom, I was usually able to get the 5-bushel daily limit by 3:00 P.M. Things went along OK for about a week and, being young and not yet very weather-wise, I suppose I became a little overconfident. Then one afternoon,

Mother Nature College enrolled me in "Winter Weather 101". An icy 40 knot WSW wind suddenly sprung up about the time I was ready to start home and it took me an hour just to get the heavily loaded boat abreast of Ram Point. I was barely able to hold my own in the puffs and had to put everything I had into gaining ground during the lulls. To make matters worse, the temperature had been dropping steadily and, with the steep chop driving the freezing spray over the bow of the rowboat, I had to pull into the lee of Sixpenny Island to bail out the skiff and knock some of the ice off the gunwales. Three weeks of steady rowing had really toughened me up, but I was definitely tiring and was starting to have serious doubts about my ability to hang in there long enough to row the rest of the way. The trip was beginning to change from just one more unpleasant job into an ordeal and I was reminded of my Dad's very difficult struggle to get down the river with the gear he salvaged from his boat after the hurricane. In the diary he described it as a "Hard Pull" but, in talking to him about it later, he admitted he had used up every bit of his reserves to get home.

My Dad's description of his trip after the hurricane was running through my mind as I was trying to decide whether to continue the struggle or to turn back, beach the boat on Willow Point and hitchhike home. I hated to give up and had made up my mind to keep plugging away until I was completely worn out or I had to bail out again to keep the boat from sinking under me. These were brave thoughts, but the skiff was icing up faster than I anticipated. I had just about decided it was time to turn around and run for shelter, when I saw one of the big Saybrook skiffs pounding down the river toward me. He had been scouting out some new scallop beds further up the river and in a few minutes he swung alongside, threw me a line and we were off in a sheet of spray. When we got back to Noank he took me aside and told me I was being penny wise and pound foolish to risk my life that way and if I was serious about scalloping during a New England winter I should get a suitably large boat and an outboard motor. The episode was actually a good lesson for me in more ways than one. I not only took his advice concerning the boat and motor, I realized for the first time that, in order to do a satisfactory job in any of life's endeavors, it is necessary to have proper equipment.

I bought a used 14 foot skiff and a nearly new 5 horse Evinrude from Harry Douglas, who then lived in Dunn's house on Pearl St, and Neil Haring kindly loaded it in her truck for me and brought it down to our dock. I was now in the big time, or so I thought, and was able to hold my end up in competition with the professionals from Saybrook. However, nothing lasts forever in the fishing business and soon we managed to put a real dent in the size of the scallop beds. My daily production began to fall off alarmingly and I was wondering what to do next, when the MacDonald brothers, Wilbur and Robert, called me on the phone one evening and offered me a site (job) as a deckhand on their nearly new dragger *KAREN & LINDA*. This was ideal for me, as they tied up at their father's fish pier at the foot of Latham Lane and I could walk to work in less than five minutes. Even more importantly, I was getting sick and tired of spending every evening opening scallops in the workshop, for it was deadly monotonous and

On my way home from bay scalloping, 1946.

was simply devastating my social life. So it was with a sigh of relief I wrapped up the bay scalloping and turned into a draggerman.

Working on someone else's boat, especially a dragger, was a big change for me, as all my prior experience had been lobstering and handlining with my Dad but, after a few trips, I settled into the routine and enjoyed the opportunity to learn another facet of the business of being a waterman. The *KAREN & LINDA* was a typical wooden, western rigged side-trawler approximately 54 feet long, with a 6 cylinder Lathrop diesel in the engine room. The engine was one of the old style, slow turning (800 RPM) units that Lathrop had converted to diesel from one of their heavy-duty gas engines and was really just a longer, dieselized version of the old 3 cylinder chugger in my Dad's lobsterboat. *KAREN & LINDA'S* rig and fishing gear were typical of a Stonington style dragger of that day, which is to say it would now be considered pretty primitive compared to the net reels and long steel ground-cables almost universally used today. In that era we had to contend with the steel-shod trawl doors swinging, and sometimes wildly thrashing, around from the overhead rig. Furthermore, it was necessary to hand haul and whip the rope ground cables and net in every haulback. While we did use a so-called Lazy Line to bring the cod end alongside, in rough weather it was a miserable and sometimes hazardous job to get the ground cables and net aboard.

As we approach the end of the 90s, otter trawling (dragging) is often described in some quarters as a non-selective, destructive method that does considerable harm to the resource by catching too many unmarketable and undersized target species, which must then be discarded dead. When I signed on aboard *KAREN & LINDA* in early December 1946, fish were so plentiful most concerns about discards centered on the labor involved in sorting through them. The fact that you could never be sure what would be in the net when it was brought aboard was

KAREN & LINDA *at MacDonald's dock at foot of Latham Lane, about 1950.*
Photo courtesy of Robert S. Palmer.

one of the most interesting aspects of the method and, being an inquisitive young man, I always enjoyed examining the variety of marine life we captured. Not that there was always time to carefully pick through the pile and examine any odd-ball thing in a scientific manner, far from it. There was a tremendous run of cod-fish, mackerel and herring along the Rhode Island beaches and outside of Fishers Island during the winter of 1946-1947, and many times we would barely have one tow picked up, washed and stowed in the hold before it was time to haul back again. This really kept your nose to the grindstone, so to speak, for when I start-ed work on the *KAREN & LINDA* the codfish run was at its peak. By going as close to the rocks on Watch Hill Reef as we dared, it was not uncommon for us to get 350 to 500 cod (most of which were steakers and had to be headed as well as gutted) plus 5 or 6 bushels of winter flounders (locally called flatfish) in a one hour tow at daybreak. Catches usually dropped off a bit after that first tow but, for the several weeks the run was on, each haulback seldom produced less than 100 cod for each hour the net was on the bottom.

After codfishing slacked off we put more effort into catching mackerel and butterfish and, while we never set any records, we had better than average success at it. The problem with catching mackerel was there were a lot of sea herring around which had virtually no value at the time. Having to pick through 5000 or 6000 pounds of herring every tow in order to salvage 20 to 30 bushels of mackerel and 5 to 10 bushels of butterfish turns into a back-breaking job very quickly, especially with only two men free to work on deck most of the time. I say two men because, even today, when you are dragging back of the reef and along the beaches east of Watch Hill, there are a lot of hang-ups and strong tides to contend with. Someone had to be at the wheel almost every minute to keep an eye on the ranges (today everyone uses loran or GPS) in order to wiggle through the obstructions on the bottom without tearing up the net.

All things considered, between fishing locally and offshore of Long Island for yellowtails, we had a pretty good winter. The MacDonald brothers were very good to work for and, for the most part, peace and harmony reigned. There were exceptions to this of course, such as getting hung up solid while towing with the tide when it was running over 3 knots or catching an ostensibly live mine; both of which took place. Hanging up in a screaming tide when you already have almost all your wire out, while not uncommon in the area we fished, can be a stressful experience but, for sheer gut tightening drama, it would take a awful lot to match catching what you have good reason to believe is a live mine.

The mine incident took place only a few weeks after the Point Judith dragger *JANE LORRAINE* had her stern blown off (fortunately with no loss of life)by a mine she had caught in her net, so we were acutely aware of the danger. We never

My first job on a dragger with Robert and Wilbur MacDonald on their KAREN & LINDA, 1946.
Photo courtesy of Robert S. Palmer.

knew for certain if the object we captured was a live mine or one of the unexploded depth charges the navy had dropped during the war. In either case, when we looked over the side and saw what was obviously a piece of military ordnance caught in the mouth of the net, instead of the rock we had thought was weighting it down, the situation had the potential of becoming extremely hazardous to our continued existence. We were squarely on the horns of a dilemma, for we didn't want to sacrifice the nearly new net by unshackling it from the doors if it was a dummy mine or a dud depth charge but, at the same time, we didn't dare hoist it up enough to cut a hole in the net. Bringing it aboard was not even considered. After some consultation between the two brothers, we very, very carefully slacked the gear off until we figured the mine was about half way to bottom and then went ahead slowly to get the net astern of us at what we hoped was a safe distance. We had only towed it a few minutes, when the boat gave a lurch and then began to move ahead at a faster rate, indicating to us the mine had torn its way through the net and we were rid of it. It would be nice to say we marked the spot so the object could be recovered, but this took place before loran was available and land was not within sight. I believe the general location was reported to the authorities and, up until a few years ago it was still shown on charts as a x marking "Reported Unexploded Ordnance".

The winter I spent with the two MacDonald brothers was a good education for me and broadened my horizons to include another way of making a living from the sea. By the end of the following year, my Dad and I had rerigged the *ANNA R* to go dragging and tub trawling during the winter months, and we spent the next few years doing just that. As for the *KAREN & LINDA*, the brothers split up a few years later, Robert to work ashore and Wilbur to go lobstering alone in a 40 foot Novie, at which time they sold the big boat. I lost track of it until 1987, when I ran across her in a Point Judith boatyard where she was hauled out for painting. In spite of suffering from over 40 years of hard service and considerable neglect, the hull appeared fairly sound, although there was extensive rot in the ice-hold sheathing and along the bulwarks. With the owner's permission, I poked around for a while and allowed my mind to wander back to 1946 in order to relive the past for a few minutes. She was certainly old, very tired and definitely obsolete, but when I left her for what was probably the last time, I gave the old girl a farewell pat on the topsides and wished her good luck.

Chapter Seventeen

EVEN WHEN YOU ARE NOT LISTENING, SOMETIMES YOU LEARN

ANNA R II *rigged for dragging. John on bow, I'm on rail, about 1948.*

Anyone who has worked for his father, as I did for 16 years, knows the true meaning of the term mixed emotions. The relations between a father and his son are almost never easy even under the best of circumstances and, when you are employed as your old man's deckhand from the age of 14 until you are 30, it certainly has its ups and downs, to say the least. In my case, my father had been dead for nearly 20 years and I had reached 50 years of age before I was secure enough in my own mind to take time to think the matter through in a non-judgmental manner and realize what a pain in the neck I must have been to him on many occasions. This was not entirely my fault, any more than it is exclusively the fault of our own kids when they are baffled by our attitudes and just cannot understand where we are coming from. It's simply the age old generation gap, which really goes into high gear when the two of you are cooped up together on a small boat for 14 to 18 hours a day, year after year.

I now appreciate the inevitability and reasons for the discord, as I hope my own son, who also worked for me on a boat for ten years, will someday realize. I say inevitability, for I have never heard of a male offspring between the ages of 13 and 30 who thought his old man had enough smarts to come in out of the rain. As a matter of fact, now that I am a parent, I know it's hard to tell if they are getting smarter or you are getting stupider, at least in their opinion. Furthermore, when you add to this the complication of a captain/deckhand hierarchy the issues become even more confused. The friction between a captain and his deckhand, especially if it is his son, is usually the *Straw that breaks the camel's back*, to quote an old saying. Even if it is not his son, it is an undeniable fact of human nature that almost every experienced deckhand tends to second-guess the captain to some extent when all does not go well, especially when the skipper makes a bonehead move.

My Dad and I used to discuss and often argue about almost every topic imaginable, from the day-to-day work aboard the boat to sports and politics. Our exchange of views was not only permitted but, as long as it did not interfere with our catch, was encouraged in what I now know was an attempt by him to stimulate my thinking. Be that as it may, there were strict rules, limits and conditions to our relationship beyond which it was very imprudent to venture. The first cardinal rule and by far the most important was to not knowingly disobey an order if he gave it with that "certain" tone in his voice. Now please don't ask me what I mean by a "certain" tone for, once you had heard it, there was never again the slightest doubt in your mind what it was. The second rule was that I should never fail to be properly prepared for the day's activity. This usually concerned either the lines, baits, nets or harpoon gear and, when he found me remiss in my duties in that department, I was probably "in for it" all the rest of the day. The opening salvo of the lecture would usually begin with the following declaration: "I absolutely refuse to keep reminding you to do something that we have to do every day." I soon learned that no matter how tired or sick I was, in the long run it was definitely the lesser of two evils to have everything ready to go when we reached the grounds.

Being tired or sick brings up another fact of life at sea, namely, that old bugaboo seasickness. Almost everyone who works on the water for a living suffers from seasickness at one time or another, although some people will never admit it, even to themselves and blame it on hangovers, migraine headaches or other ills. When you stop and think about it, it's self evident that once in awhile you are going to have an upset stomach no matter where you happen to be and, if you are working aboard a boat on a day that you would be sick if you were home, you are darn well going to be sick on the boat; case closed. Personally, I know a lot more about seasickness than anybody really needs to know, for I got seasick every time

ANNA R II *returning from fishing grounds. I'm aft mending the net, 1949.*
Photographer: Al Haring.

it got rough during the first two or three years of my apprenticeship. In my case, being sick at my stomach was not considered an excuse, let alone a reason, to knock off work, lay down on the deck and moan pitifully. It wasn't that my Dad didn't know the meaning of the word sympathy. He knew it was somewhere in the dictionary. He even claimed he had looked it up one day and found it some-where between sh** and symphony. It's just that he felt stopping work because you were seasick had no place aboard a small fishing boat.

The upshot of his work ethic was, short of calling in dead, one should learn to work sick or hurt at an early age. Although nowadays this would probably be classed as borderline child abuse by some overly protective types, my Dad knew from bitter experience how valuable mental toughness in the face of adversity can be to an adult. He would never berate me when I was seasick, but would wipe me off, pat me on the head and quietly say something like "Now that you are through throwing up, it's time to get back to work and cut some more bait for us." The first time this happened I thought he was the worst person in the world to treat me in that manner, and told my Mom as much when we got home that afternoon. She was properly sympathetic and said she would take it up with my Dad and have him ease up on me. I never found out if she did this or not, but a few days later my Dad had one of his infamous bilious attacks and was a whole lot sicker than I had ever been. When I saw him heaving his guts out while we were handlining cod and never missing a stroke as long as the bite was on, I was determined to show him I could be just as tough as he was.

To keep working when you are violently seasick is not an easy task for an adult, let alone a 14 year old kid, for you feel simply AWFUL, especially when you are sick in the morning. Your stomach is churning, your head is spinning and you just know that the boat will continue to gyrate up and down for hours to come. Learning how to keep plugging away when I felt terrible was a hard struggle but, as so often happened, my Dad turned out to be right in the end. His example has stood me in good stead all the rest of my life and many times has enabled me to keep going when every fiber in my body was screaming at me to give up and quit.

Like many watermen, my Dad was something of a philosopher and, given the slightest opportunity, would expound at great length on what he considered to be basic maritime rules. Several of these he claimed, and I now feel rightly so, are of value beyond the marine sphere and might be successfully applied to other life situations. Depending on your personal outlook, some of them may be considered old fashioned and wrong headed as we fast approach the 21st century, but here they are anyway. By the way, you should bear in mind that, even today, the average commercial fishing operation is not run under the precepts of democracy. Its participants are not normally subject to any collective bargaining agreements, minimum wage, overtime pay, sick or vacation days, company health insurance or retirement benefits. As a matter of fact, the operation is probably closer to a benevolent dictatorship than any other known form of management.

Here are three of my Dad's basic marine rules.

Rule #1. The captain is in charge and fully responsible for the operation of the vessel at all times AND THERE IS ONLY ROOM FOR ONE CAPTAIN ON A BOAT. My Dad would go on to say, "This is not a college debating society and we are not going to run this operation by a committee. On the other hand, I am

Dad knitting a net in our livingroom, about 1949.

always open to suggestions and new ideas, but I will make the final decision based on my greater experience. Furthermore, you are not required to agree with me or even like it, but you will have only two choices: do it, or quit. If you want to run a boat, buy a boat, and then you can make your own mistakes." He would then declare, "Owning a fishing boat gives you the privilege of being wrong and paying through the nose for the error of your ways."

Rule #2. It is absolutely necessary that everyone makes adequate preparation for the normal daily work schedule and each person is expected to help maintain the equipment properly. As I mentioned before, my Dad had next to no patience with anybody who wasn't ready when we reached the grounds and utter contempt for those who let things go until they broke from lack of care. He was also a firm believer in having enough spares; "If you can't run or fish without it, you had better carry a spare for it, if possible," he declared more times than I like to remember. Therefore we carried points, plugs, impellers, spare carburetor parts, gasket material, hose clamps, a selection of the various hoses used on the engine and an assortment of nuts and bolts. However, lest you think he went overboard on the subject, we never carried any spares we were not able to make use of while we were at sea.

Rule #3. DO IT THE RIGHT WAY. This sounds pretty simple on the surface, but it entailed far more than the ability to perform a mechanical task in a proscribed manner. Although doing things properly the first time was the primary basis for the statement, he considered that the maxim also included dealing with your fellow man in an honorable manner and not engaging in underhanded tactics, outright cheating or blatantly illegal activities to get ahead in life. He continually pointed out examples of unacceptable and outright criminal actions that eventually brought down the mighty. "Ill gotten gains never stick to you and can never bring you the contentment that is vitally important for a full life," he would intone. Then he would go on to tell of what happened to some of his acquaintances who had profited well during prohibition from Rum Running, but who either ended up as drunks or had other misfortunes which kept them from enjoying the fruits of their labors.

He was also quite free with fishing information and, other than protecting some spots that could only support a single boat, kept very few professional secrets. He firmly believed that no person is smart enough to be a world beater every day and everybody needs help from time to time as they blunder their way through life. "No individual has all the good ideas, and you should be alert to those of others and see if they can be used for your benefit," was another of his words of advice to me. He was also a firm believer in returning something to society and, if needed, to individuals as you grew older. "When you are young, you often have to accept freely given help from others that you can't really return in kind. It may even be embarrassing to you to accept it under those circumstances, but do so in the spirit in which it is given. Just remember, life always comes full circle and someday it will be your turn to give freely with no hope of any return." He would then go on to say, "When it is your turn to give, remember to also pass on this advice to ensure the chain of a good lifestyle is not broken. The only sin in accepting such a gift when you are young is the failure to return the gift, in all probability not to the original giver, but to some other young person in need." He had an old-fashioned sort of morality which might be sneered at by many of the present generation but, in retrospect, it has benefited me greatly as opportunities have arisen that enabled me to put some of his advice into practice. I feel that, far from being out of the mainstream of the 90s, the precept of passing on his beliefs on human conduct, not just by words, but by example and deed, is one of the keys to helping man to live peaceably with his fellow man.

Although my Dad was rather short tempered and likely to blow up with only slight provocation, he could be remarkably patient with me if he thought I was doing my best. In this regard he would seldom chew me out the FIRST time I made a mistake, but woe betide me if I made the same error twice. He taught me that most first-time errors should be treated as learning experiences and an intelligent person can often turn them into valuable tools in understanding a given problem. Repeating the same mistake, however, was an indication of either stupidity or lack of attention and, while he never accused me of being in competition with Einstein, he did consider me to be trainable. His usual verdict when I had screwed up again was simply that I was just not applying the level of intelligence I had been blessed with and needed the benefit of one more lecture about concentrating more fully on the task at hand. For someone my age, this requirement was a pretty tall order, especially when you consider that very few normal teenage males are able to focus their attention for more than a few moments on any area above their belt buckle. My Dad knew this well, but he never let it deter him from trying to divert my attention from my lower pelvis to my brain.

Another axiom propounded at every opportunity was his unshakable opinion that simplicity in both boat construction and problem solving were paramount virtues for successfully operating a fishing boat. His approach when some piece of equipment broke or did not work properly was to start with the simplest reason for the failure FIRST and work your way up from there. Sounds self evident, doesn't it, but you would be surprised how often people fail to use simple common sense, especially in an emergency. Another opinion he drilled into me was that in fitting out any type of boat, one should never, never install anything absolutely necessary for the operation of the vessel in a location which would require something else to be removed before you could service the critical part. Things such as water pump impellers that cannot be replaced quickly and easily because they are virtually impossible to reach were a definite no-no as far as he was concerned.

Unfortunately, except for the builders of "Downeast" lobsterboat hulls, almost all fiberglass boat builders are now only a division of a large industrial conglomerate, wherein styling and the bottom line are the governing factors in most designs and how to fix anything has a very low priority. While shoe-horning essential machinery into place with only inches to spare is sometimes necessary, there is seldom a valid reason for their attempts to cram 10 cubic feet of nonessential gear into 5 cubic feet of space. As a marine surveyor who examines about 100+ boats a year, I am continually distressed to find my Dad's basic principles are all too often ignored by a substantial number of the present-day boat manufacturers. I have often thought that if boat builders were required to share the labor costs for the normal maintenance of their product for several years after purchase, they would soon find ways to leave room for ready access to components.

Another valuable lesson from my Dad was connected to the fact that in those days we were still limited to what I call "The Joshua Slocum Methods" of coastwise navigation and pilotage, using only the chart, the compass and the alarm clock (we actually used a wrist watch). While this may seem to be archaic in this electronic age, it was all we had to work with, other than an infrequently used sounding lead. Instead of the present notebooks full of loran bearings, like every fisherman of that era, we compiled notebooks full of ranges and depths for fishing grounds, as well as courses and running times to and from any place we might possibly need to go during flood, ebb and slack water conditions. My Dad was a stickler for steering a compass course and double checking our running time each and every time we went anywhere. That way, if it shut in thick of fog, he knew that the courses and times were as close to correct as was humanly possible. In those not so long ago days, before depthsounders, loran and finally radar became available in small enough packages for a 30 foot boat, you had to have this information at your fingertips so you could run your time out with confidence that you would be able to see or hear your next mark when you shut down. Losing your nerve and shutting down before you had run your time out were just not acceptable for that type of navigation, and you quickly found out you had to have the courage of your convictions if you were going to survive.

You also developed an acute sense of your own position relative to important landmarks, especially offshore when you were out of sight of land for many hours. Out there you were often charging about all day, hither and yon in haze and fog, searching for swordfish and/or tuna. In foggy weather you usually tried to go east and west or north and south for a set time to simplify matters. This was a good theory but seldom worked out completely, especially when you hooked a large tuna or ironed a swordfish that took you a considerable distances on an oblique course. More than one boat lost track of their wanderings on a foggy day and wound up many miles from where they thought they would be, when they finally made the land. Today, being restricted to that type of navigation is far in the past and most of the old timers limited to those primitive tools are long-since gone to whatever reward watermen are destined to receive. Nevertheless, the basic skills we learned are still applicable today, albeit seldom utilized in this electronic age where one hesitates to leave the dock on a foggy day if the radar is inoperative.

It was not my plan to turn this essay into an exposition of my own personal philosophy, but this too is probably a natural extension of the teachings I assimilated from my Dad without even being aware it was taking place. As the title of this piece suggests, we were a typical New England father-son pair, with him extolling the virtues of hard work, close attention to daily details and the need for a resilient spirit in the face of adversity. Me, I was a normal teenager, who felt that the old man's mind was still firmly rooted in the preceding century and many of his ideals had been left behind by the march of time. Looking back with the crystal clear hindsight that comes with age, I now realize the guidance, advice and discipline I received from my Dad during my formative years was primarily responsible for whatever measure of success I have achieved.

One last thought, my Dad had another of his famous sayings that I must leave with you and it went like this. "There are two important decisions all of us have to make that will, in great part, determine the course of our lives. The first one is to decide when it is the proper time to start something, be it business, sports or a marriage. Even more important, and infinitely more difficult, is to decide when to stop. It is a far better thing to go out at the top of your form than to hang on too long and embarrass yourself." It would probably be a benefit to all concerned if some of our politicians and professional athletes heeded his advice.

Striped bass. Dad, John, and my son Robert and me, about 1955.

Dad, about 1946.

Chapter Eighteen

SWORDFISHING

ANNA R II *with harpooned swordfish, about 1955.*

Although broadbill swordfish are certainly no more overfished than most of the other species caught off our coasts, I have a lot of trouble viewing them in the same light as, say, cod or the flounders. Admittedly, this is a personal bias on my part, but I just cannot put them in anything other than a class by themselves. Until the development of the distant water longline fishery in the 1960s, where vessels set out up to 40 miles of baited hooks, swordfish had been primarily caught by harpooning mature fish as they cruised the surface waters of the continental shelf. The commercial harvest of swordfish by this method had been pursued for slightly more than 100 years with no noticeable decrease in the size of fish landed, being, on average, roughly 200 pounds dressed weight or approximately 300 pounds alive. Today, the longline fishery takes place throughout the entire Atlantic Ocean, with fleets from Europe and America essentially meeting in mid-ocean. The combination of increased effort and the mostly non-selective aspect of the pelagic longlines has caused the average landed weight to decline to less than 1/3 of the historical 200 pounds. Innumerable numbers of immature fish are being landed and/or discarded at sea. As could be expected, the survival rate of discarded juveniles is the subject of considerable dispute and debate with polarized positions on both sides of the issue. Anyway, whatever your feelings may be concerning swordfish longlining, it is virtually certain the inshore harpoon fishery, and way of life I pursued during the summer months for over 20 years is gone forever; period.

Although it is a truism that most commercial fishermen fish for dollars, not fish, the harpoon sword fishery was, to me and many others who engaged in it, almost an occupational disease bordering on obsession and addiction. Most of us who were bitten by the "Swordfish Bug" considered it to be the most interesting, and sometimes thrilling, fishery available to us since our forefathers gave up sallying forth to hunt the great whales. It had all the components of the primordial impulse to hunt for game and more than its share of "The thrill of victory and the agony of defeat." It included the patient search for the animal, sometimes lasting many days; the careful stalking of the unwary prey in order to get within range for the harpoon; and the elation of a successful throw by the harpooner, known in the trade as the Striker who would attempt to iron the swordfish.

On the minus side, there was the sickening feeling of missing a sucker shot and seeing your day's pay escape into the depths of the sea. Not only that, like all acts requiring a high degree of hand-eye coordination, such as baseball and golf, a Striker's "slumps" tended to feed on themself, breeding a subconscious lack of confidence and opening the door to further failures. I can tell you from bitter experience that missing two or three, or God forbid 4 or 5, easy shots in a row feels even worse than losing your high school girlfriend to the captain of the football team. Added to these normal internal recriminations, it was often necessary to put up with the outright contempt of a disgruntled crew member who would probably say something like this. "Geee-zus Cap, how in Hell did you miss that fish? I put you right ovah the top'a him an if you'da just waited a little longer you could'a just reached down and poked him instead-a throwin tha pole. Whadda-ya say Cap, how about you let me take a crack at the next one we see?" These were times to truly try one's soul to the utmost and the only saving grace was that it is impossible for a crewman to fire the captain, especially if he also owns the boat. Be that as it may, many a Striker put in a lot of very lonely days when he was having trouble hitting the target. You just had to tough it out and hope you could get back on track before the crew mutinied and chucked you overboard.

All told, I spent the first half (1946-1957) of the 20 odd years I pursued the harpoon swordfishery while working for my Dad as a Striker and the other half on my own after he passed away. Although our relatively small boats (31 and 40 feet) kept us from fishing on Georges Bank and other offshore grounds, we did OK on the local level and usually were among the top producers. Over the years, we had both adventures and misadventures, but my Dad, at least, was a very careful boat operator and when he was in command, things almost always went according to plan. He had the best "eyes" for finning swordfish of any of the men I fished with but, surprisingly, most of the time swordfishing was just part of a normal day's work to him. Not so with me, I was bitten by the swordfish bug from the outset and, for the first few years, I operated at the upper end of over-drive mode when we were offshore. There's only room for one raving maniac on a 31 foot boat, so it's a good thing my Dad was in charge and managed to keep me out of serious trouble. In that regard, the following are a few of the more inter-esting events which have stuck in my mind all these years.

One day we were cruising about a half mile from Art Coleman's *JANIE DELL* when Art came across a huge mako shark feeding on a large swordfish, which the mako had apparently just killed. Art Ironed the mako and, while he was attempt-ing to subdue the furiously struggling shark, gave us a call on the radio to see if we would come over and try to salvage what was left of the swordfish. In a few minutes we arrived on scene and, sure enough, there was what would have been a 400 pound dressed-weight swordfish being attacked by 4 or 5 good sized dusky sharks. My Dad swooped down on the thrashing mass of sharks and backed down alongside the swordfish carcass, meanwhile yelling at me to gaff up its head and try to get a rope strap on it somehow. I managed to get the head part way out of the water, but the sharks were ripping and yanking at the other end of the body in a feeding frenzy, and it was all I could do to hold onto the gaff, let alone get a rope strap on the head for the hoisting tackle.

Before I could even open my mouth to yell for assistance, my Dad was leaning over the rail with a strap in his right hand. He reached down and grabbed the swordfish's bill with his left hand, heaved it up and rammed his right hand into the fish's mouth and out the gills. He ducked one end of the loop through the other, cinched it up hard and said "Quick, unhook the gaff, hook on the tackle and grab the ballbat." In less time than it takes to tell, we were dragging what was left of the poor swordfish out of the water, while I clubbed away at the sharks still clinging tenaciously to it. Even though the sharks had eaten the tail and several feet of the body immediately adjacent, we still salvaged nearly 300 pounds of meat, which we later split 50-50 with Art as a reward for the call. We tried to sell our portion to Otto Grossman's Fish market, but he wouldn't buy a shark-bit swordfish, which was already dead when we salvaged it as he was worried about the possibility of contamination. Don't worry, it didn't go to waste, for our whole neighborhood had swordfish steaks for dinner at least once a week all winter long and nobody complained or got sick.

Another time, Don Gross of the *CAPTAIN DON*, who was strictly a rod and reel angler, called us over to see if we could harpoon a big swordfish he had been unsuccessfully attempting to catch by dragging a squid in front of it. We promised him half the fish for the accommodation, but he said he could only hang around for less than a half hour and doubted we could land it in that short a time. Did he have a surprise! I fortunately drove the brass harpoon dart right between two vertebrae, severed the spine and killed the fish on the spot. We had it alongside within 20 seconds and hoisted up, gutted and in the boat in another minute. I had the head off in rapid order, slid a rope strap under the body to find the balance point, cut the carcass in half, tied a piece of pot warp to the tail and threw the end over to the CAPTAIN DON, which had pulled on our starboard side to watch the action. My Dad and I wrestled Don's half over the side of the ANNA R and Don had it in his boat and was underway for Montauk Harbor in less than 15 minutes. While the episode hasn't been immortalized in the Guinness Book of Records, it's probably never going to be challenged, given the permanent demise of the inshore sword fishery.

When I think back on some of the things which took place while swordfishing, I have to admit we were lucky nobody got seriously injured. What was probably my closest call came when I was flipped off the swordfish pulpit. My Dad liked to go on the fish head-to-head if conditions permitted. He reasoned correctly that swordfish couldn't swim backwards and so, no matter which way a spooked fish tried to go, you had a better chance of nailing it on the way by, compared to trying to chase it if you were coming from behind. One thing for sure, whatever happened took place in a hurry and you had better be ready to throw the harpoon in a split second if the fish tried to dart away. On the day of the near accident, we had tried several times to get close enough to a swordfish for me to iron it, but each time it had sounded before we were able to get close enough for me to throw the harpoon. Luckily, each time it sounded it had popped up again in a few minutes and we would make another run at it. The ability to make two or more attempts to get within throwing range of the harpoon was not unusual in those days of swordfish abundance and, following his customary practice, my Dad increased our boat speed each time we made another approach.

What turned out to be the final run was therefore made at our full cruising speed of 8+ knots. The fish was paddling along towards us at a couple knots as we went surging towards it and, like before, it started to settle away. I got off a desperate throw at the limit of my range and saw the iron strike home just behind the head. At the same instant, the fish porpoised up out of the water toward the boat and the 14 foot wooden harpoon pole came shooting back over the top of the swordfish "stand" attached to the end of the pulpit. The butt end of the pole struck me just under the breastbone and catapulted me backwards over the top of the guy wires which served as a railing running from the bow to the "stand." Fortunately, I made a lucky grab and caught the port guy wire with my right hand as I went flipping over it. Somehow or other, I managed to hang on as I completed my arc and slammed into the side of the 2X10" fir plank. The boat was still moving forward at a good clip and, hanging as I was from the wire, my legs were immersed above the knees, and I was almost dragged under the boat. Fortunately, I hung on until the boat had lost headway, then painfully hauled myself back aboard. Oh yes, we got the fish.

After my Dad died in 1958, I concentrated more than ever on swordfishing and in 1960, when I finally launched the 40 foot wooden Walter McInnes sportfisherman my Dad and I had begun building, I went at it as hard as I could. I purchased a new 13 foot dory for $125.00, which Perry Durea had brought down from Nova Scotia on one of his lobster carriers, and when we went 3-handed, we would tow it behind the big boat so the third man could tend the harpooned fish from it and free the powerboat to continue searching. Although I doubt any of us were aware of it at the time, the next few years were to be the grand finale of the inshore fishery for swordfish, both recreational and commercial. While I am eternally grateful to have participated in this last hurrah, it is also saddening to realize that none of our grandchildren will ever have the opportunity to see the annual migration of these magnificent fish. Many days in the 1960s we would see 5 or 6 fish, their distinctive sickle-shaped fins cutting the surface of the water and, on two occasions, we saw between 30 and 40 "finning-out" in a 2 hour period. During those two days we were in a virtual frenzy, with 4 or 5 fish visible at a time, most of which were wild as a hawk and very hard to approach.

The first time this took place, we hadn't seen a swordfish in 9 straight days and were, frankly, getting pretty discouraged. There was a cold 20 knot NW wind blowing that morning and it was downright miserable. We were slatting and banging around in the steep chop and, up until about 10:30, we hadn't seen a thing. As a matter of fact, my mate, Pete Homan, and I were discussing giving it up as a bad chance and going home to save fuel. By 11:00 A.M. the wind died completely, the water had slicked-off and there were swordfish fins everywhere we looked. We were only 2-handed, so had left the dory home that morning, but we managed to iron 7 fish in the next two hours and, for the first time in my life we had all of our five kegs, each of which was attached to the end of a 50 fathom warp, out simultaneously. Having harpooned swordfish towing 5 kegs in as many directions is both good and bad, for there is no guarantee the fish will not change direction and many a sword fisherman has lost track of kegs when they ended up miles apart. We managed to keep track of them, albeit with considerable difficulty, and ended the day with 5 fish ranging from 185 to 390 pounds dressed weight.

Another aspect of the swordfish harpoon fishery was the possibility of having a wounded and enraged swordfish attack either the boat or the dory. We experienced both. The *ANNA R's* bottom was pierced by a wild fish we had briefly stunned and were trying to get a tail-rope on before it came-to. I had struck it just behind the head and when we had pulled it up within about 30 feet it turned towards us and went swooping right under the boat. There was a loud bang, the fish stopped struggling and we quickly pulled up the tail and got a strap on it. When we got the fish aboard we noticed that about 6 inches of the sword was broken off, but a quick examination of the bilges did not show any obvious leak so we figured the swordfish had probably struck the keel while trying to escape. However, when we hauled out for winter storage, we discovered a piece of the sword sticking out of the planking just below the turn of the bilge. We had been trying to pin down a slow but annoying leak all fall and there it was at last. The sword had entered the planking at an acute angle and the part which pierced the

Large swordfish, about 1955.

One of my happy days.

Rod and reel caught swordfish on ANNA R III.
I'm on the left, Chuck Doughty, former owner of
the Seahorse Tavern, on the right, 1963.

Average sized harpooned swordfish. Daughter Beth
Ann on bridge, mate Pete Homan on right, 1963.

hull was between the interior sheathing and the planking and therefore impossible to see. I could not get enough of a purchase on the stub to pull the fragment out, so just ground it back a little below the surface of the planking and patched the area with Marine Tex.

The second ramming was much more exciting and there was no doubt concerning what took place. Fortunately, on that day, my deckhand Pete Homan and I were augmented by my son Franklin, Walt Maynard and Chuck Doughty, the former owner of the "Seahorse Tavern." I had ironed a good-sized swordfish which took off like an express train across the surface for a few hundred yards and then began thrashing about and beating the water to a froth with its sword. I put my deckhand, Pete Homan, in the dory and told him to be careful and take it easy until the fish quieted down. The advice was probably unnecessary for it didn't take a genius to know he was going to be dealing with a dangerous swordfish. We started off in the *ANNA R* after a breaching swordfish about a half mile away, which we had spotted while dropping off the dory but, as could be expected, kept a close watch on Pete's situation in case something went wrong.

In about 10 minutes, I could see that the swordfish was no longer careening around on the surface and the doryman appeared to be slowly retrieving the 50 fathoms of warp between the keg and the swordfish. We were cruising around looking for signs of the breacher when I noticed a lot of commotion back at the dory and could see Pete flailing away with one of the oars at something inside the dory. We cranked the 6/71 up to All Ahead, Battle and, as we got closer, we could see Pete perched on the stem of the dory. The keg was about 100 yards away and being towed at a good clip to windward. Pete was soaking wet and obviously shook-up, but unhurt. The dory was half full of water and there was a ragged 3/4" X 2" hole in both sides near the stern about 2" above the bottom. It turned out the swordfish had come porpoising toward the dory at what Pete claimed was nearly 40 miles an hour and had driven his sword in one side and out through the other. There was real danger that the violently gyrating swordfish would upset the dory and dump Pete into the sea, so he grabbed an oar and flailed away at the sword until he broke it off and freed the fish. By then he could see us racing toward him, so he climbed up into the bow to keep the holes near the stern out of water to prevent the dory from swamping.

Other than the two holes, the dory was undamaged so I grabbed a couple of rags and a screwdriver, jumped down into the dory and jammed the rags tightly into the gaps in the planking. I climbed back aboard the *ANNA R* and said, "OK guys, Pete's going back in the dory to get me that fish while I go look for the breacher. Which one of you wants to volunteer to go along with him and bail?" There was no immediate response so I simply ushered Chuck over to the rail and said, "Get in Chuck, you're IT." I know he really didn't want to get into that damaged dory and go after the swordfish, but on the other hand, I was the captain and he didn't want to "Chicken Out" on what was more of a direct order than a request. His reluctance was understandable, but to his credit, he went anyway. Fortunately the swordfish had worn itself out in the attack and within 15 minutes they had it alongside the dory and tailroped.

In the 20 years I spent swordfishing there were many other episodes which I could relate in detail if space permitted. They would include getting 16 swordfish in 7 days with only a 10-year old boy (Bart Crossman) for a deckhand; trying several times to harpoon breachers in midair when they jumped just as I was getting ready to iron them (I missed every time) and losing a stunned fish that "came-to" when we tried to boat it immediately. An angry swordfish is astonishingly strong and that particular one managed to take the tailrope away from the mate, broke 3 gaffs we were trying to hold him with and, as a final gesture, gave me a black eye with his tail before tearing loose and escaping when the warp caught around the bill of a swordfish we had lying on deck.

Although we didn't know it at the time, looking back on it, those were glory days and I now know how the Plains Indians must have felt after the immense herds of buffalo were essentially exterminated by the white hunters. Like the buffalo, swordfish may possibly recover somewhat under the international quotas and regulations now in place, but it is totally illogical to presume they will EVER recover enough for a worthwhile inshore harpoon fishery of mature females to reoccur. In my opinion, it just ain't gonna happen. Unfortunately, short of a calamity that, God forbid, sets civilization back 500 years, I think it's safe to say that the way of life I pursued as an inshore swordfish harpooner is gone forever.

Jack Wilbur's STAR *towing* ANNA R II *to Lathrop's for engine repairs. Both are rigged for swordfishing, 1950s. Photographer: AL Haring*

Chapter Nineteen

Some Memorable Captains and Events

Thinking back over nearly a lifetime on the water, it occurred to me that I ought to record some of the goings-on and incidents connected with a few of the other captains I knew during my career. Some of these stories stand out in my mind because the protagonists were totally unlike what you would normally see around the waterfront today, others are humorous in an odd sort of way and, finally, some are stories of near disasters carrying a message for all who venture on the water.

I remember Captain Sherman, but I don't remember his first name as he wasn't around for more than a couple of summers. He was one of a group of semi-itinerant charter boat captains who used to come north in the summer and return to sail out of Florida in the winter. Being somewhat of a loner, he was only a casual acquaintance of my Dad. It is also well to remember that this was back in the days before enclosed flying bridges came into use and the radio, if there was one, was normally kept down in the cabin where it was dry and was, at least in some cases, only turned on to eavesdrop on the more voluble skippers. Thus, you only had a waving acquaintance with many of the other operators even though you might have fished alongside of them for several years.

This was true in spades for Sherman. Although he had an antenna bolted to the side of his bridge and therefore owned a marine radio, he never talked to another boat while on the grounds. We knew, however, that he or his mate listened all the time, for no sooner had fish been reported by another boat in the fleet than old Sherman would be headed in that direction as fast as he could. Naturally, this conduct did not endear him to most of the other captains, for although the information was given freely over a public channel and available to all, nobody appreciates a one-way type of guy who uses everybody, but does not contribute anything himself. Come to think of it, we still have some of these types around today and they are no better liked than Sherman was in his day.

The resentment towards Sherman was further compounded by the fact that he was an outsider to begin with and, having a fancy yacht-like boat compared to most of the others in the fleet, tended to suck up whatever big-money tourists were wandering around the waterfront shopping for a fishing trip. This didn't bother us too much, for in the immediate post-war era we were primarily lobstering and dragging and only took charters on a part time basis or to fill-in during slow periods in the other fisheries. However, in the case of Sherman, the combination of ingredients definitely generated a considerable amount of hate and discontent among the captains in New London where Sherman docked.

For those who are too young to remember the 1940s and 50s, I ought to clarify what I meant by a fancy, yacht-like boat. Back in the dim past when these events took place, with the exception of Glen Gordon's *MARIETTA*, 95% of the other charterboats in the local fleet were either single engine, gasoline powered, semi-converted workboats or ancient reconstructed, low end pleasure boats, none of which had much beyond a bare minimum of creature comforts. Sherman, by contrast, had a fairly new yacht (I think it was a Matthews or a Richardson) with an enclosed deckhouse, dinette, galley and, wonder of wonders, foam rubber berth cushions. Almost all the other boats had a home-built flybridge, plain wood bunk bottoms with a life preserver for a pillow and Calcutta bamboo outriggers. Sherman had a factory built flybridge with guyed double spreader outriggers that had been designed by Tommy Gifford. Not only that, he had twin Buda diesels for power and could speed along at the blinding speed of 12 knots compared to the 8 to 10 knots that was the average for the rest of the local gang. Even more distressing was the fact that he was known to slash his prices to whatever extent he felt would be necessary to underbid any of the other boats. Needless to say, his popularity was not high when be blew in from Florida in a blaze of glory, and it declined rapidly.

This introduction is meant to provide some background for the substance of my tale which, I hope, will be instructive on how not to succeed in the charterboat business. To get to the point, the episode I am going to relate began on a beautiful July day sometime around 1949 when the fleet, including the *ANNA R* with my Old Man at the helm and yours truly as deckhand, was trolling for medium size bluefin tuna about 16 miles south of Montauk Point. On the way out that morning, my Dad decided to play a hunch, and instead of heading south of Montauk Point toward where we had fished the day before, he took advantage of a strong ebb tide to go south from Endeavor Shoals buoy, and we ended up about five miles east of the fleet. No sooner had we crossed the line where the cool green inshore water changed to the warmer blue of the ocean than we came across a huge school of 30 to 50 lb. tuna on top, pushing water. We swung ahead of the school, hooked up on all four rods plus two handlines and, as often happened if you were the first boat on a big school, were able to jig about half a hundred bluefin on our first stop. After the first few minutes it was obvious we were going to get all the fish we needed so my Dad put a call out over the radio and the rush was on. As more and more boats zeroed in on them, the school began to break up a bit, but the bite was still on and soon there were about 15 boats within a mile radius trying desperately to get their load before it quit entirely.

Sherman, as it turned out, had developed a fuel problem from a clogged filter on the way out and was the last to arrive. Like any charterboat captain arriving late on the grounds from a preventable mechanical problem, he was naturally under the gun from his customers to catch up, and I expect that everyone aboard was a little jumpy. Most of the time, when you get to a school-tuna bite as it is dwindling away from boat pressure, the hardest step is to hook the first fish. After you overcome that hurdle, it is critical for your continuing success to keep both the angler and the deckhand from screwing up bad enough to lose the fish. This was especially true when you got the tuna almost to the boat, as back then there were often many other tuna following it that you could jig up. Briefly stated, the idea was to reel the hooked fish almost to the boat and then swim it along while the rest of your customers jigged in the wake behind it. Sometimes there were only a few curiosity seekers following the hooked fish, but I have also had an entire 100 ton school behind the boat and baled well over 150 of them before we quit when we ran out of room. The danger lay in losing the original fish, in which case it was likely the rest would follow it down and you would be back to square one.

We were only a couple of hundred yards away fighting a small fish on light tackle when Sherman finally brought his first tuna to the boat, accompanied by a volley of bellowed instructions from the captain to his well dressed but obviously inexperienced customers. Under the baleful eye of my Dad, I was preoccupied by our own angler and missed the initial screw-up. However, it is a truism that passengers on a charterboat usually pay much more attention to what is going on aboard adjacent boats than what is taking place on their boat, so our passengers treated me to a running account of the events that took place. As near as I recall, it went like this. "Looks like they've got a big one on over there mate. I sure would like to get a big one like that to top off these small ones. Boy, that's a nice looking boat that guy's got over there, does he take parties on it? What dock does he run out of Cap? Are those diesel engines he's got there mate? What makes them smoke so much? Hey Cap, how many fish does he have so far? You say he takes it down to Florida in the winter. Say Cap, why don't you do that? (sotto voice to one of his companions) Hey Joe, look at the size of those reels he's got over there. (now back to the mate) How come his outriggers are so much longer than ours and have all those wire guys on them? (from our tiring angler) Cap, I think there's something wrong with my reel, my drag is slipping and I can't keep the line from going out." All these comments are par for the course.

By this time we had brought our fish to the gaff and, as we already had all the tuna we needed and my Old Man's kidneys were floating, we laid-to for a minute while he went below to relieve the pressure. Sherman's sweating angler now had the double line up and the mate was readying himself at the rail with the gaff. His customers (everyone took at least 7 or 8 passengers in those days before the 6-pack rule) were all milling about in the rather small cockpit, crowding around the fighting chair and urging the angler to PUMP at the top of their lungs. Sherman was still bellowing instructions that added to the din and the mate was unsuccessfully trying to clear the customers out of the way to get at the fish. Just as the swivel between the end of the fishline and the 6-foot wire leader appeared, the fish abruptly reversed direction and swam rapidly across the stern. The mate took a wild swipe at it with the gaff but missed. Sherman gave a screech that could be heard a mile away. All the customers surged to the stern to see what was up and the mate joined the chorus by yelling at the poor angler to "Pump, Damn it, Pump!" The fish, it looked like a 40 to 50 pounder, hadn't taken much line but, as often happens on charterboats with two fighting chairs, one port and one starboard, and no center chair, the fish had quickly circled around to the other side of the boat and the line was leading over the rail on the opposite side from the chair.

A general struggle then took place to jackass the angler over to the other chair. The mate strong-armed the rod away from the angler, who fought tooth and nail to retain his death grip on it. Several of the other customers helped the angler change chairs and the mate, after taking several ferocious pumps, returned the rod to the now thoroughly disturbed angler. The poor guy was obviously getting tired out from fighting the fish, tireder yet of the ribbing he was getting from his friends and even more tired of being berated by both the captain and the mate. Up comes the swivel again; another wild swipe with the gaff which dug a deep groove in the varnished mahogany transom but missed the fish by a mile; followed by another dash across the transom by the tuna and more of the captain's profanity. By this time there were so many people around the chair that it could not swivel around, and the rod was jerked upward smashing the angler right on the end of the nose. The mate made a mad dash across the boat and, reaching far underwater, managed to catch the tuna in the tail with the gaff. Meanwhile someone, nobody would own up to it afterward, threw the reel into free spool. The tuna still had his tail underwater and was dragging the mate aft as it struggled furiously to escape. About then the mate tripped over a customer he had knocked down in his haste and dropped the gaff. The fish, gaff still firmly implanted, plunged towards freedom and the line began to peel off the reel. However, the reel, now being in free spool, promptly backlashed, smashing the angler in the nose a second time. The line parted with a loud report and the fish and the gaff disappeared into the depths.

While this Chinese fire drill was taking place, Captain Sherman had moved to the back of the flybridge to get a better view of the action and increased the volume of his tirade. Now that the fish was gone, he continued to curse and yell at both the mate and the charter at the top of his lungs, getting increasingly personal in his attack. This went on for a couple of minutes until the mate finally had a bellyful of being blamed for something that was not entirely his fault. He stopped cursing at the customers, turned around and directed his venom at the captain. Their heated exchange went back and forth several times, increasing in tempo, until the mate lost his cool completely, gave a leap across the cockpit and bounded up the flybridge ladder two rungs at a time. Sherman met him at the top of the ladder with a slap across the mouth that would have stunned a horse, but the mate had his Irish up by that time and he just kept right on coming. Both he and the captain were big, burly Crunch and Des type characters, and they proceeded to duke it out like a couple of middleweight contenders.

My Dad had seen enough of this display and steered the ANNA R over to Sherman's boat. My Dad was also no slouch at bellowing and when he let loose with a, "Hey You Two Knuckleheads!" they were both shocked into inaction. He then continued, "If you two don't stop fighting immediately, I'm going to notify the Coast Guard and make sure that you both are brought up on charges." Neither of them said a word in reply to the threat, but it brought both of them to their senses. The mate went back down into the cockpit and Sherman went forward to the wheel, threw the boat into gear and took off toward Montauk in a cloud of diesel smoke. The episode was not quite over for Sherman however, for the unfortunate angler brought his tale of woe to the attention of the dockmaster at Marster's, where Sherman kept his boat. What happened after that was never made public, but I do know the other captains had already complained bitterly to the marina manager about Sherman's previous infractions. It was no surprise, when several weeks later, Captain Sherman and his boat suddenly left the area, never to return.

Another memorable captain went by the name of Hooker. I'll have to admit that, during the several years we fished near him, we never knew his full name or even if Hooker was simply a nickname. He just showed up one spring and when my Dad yelled over to Bert Stevens and asked who he was, Bert replied, "Hooker." "Hooker who?" shot back my Dad. Bert gave a shrug and replied "I dun-no, Hooker's all I know him by," and that was that, at least till the end of our association with him. Hooker was one of a number of commercial hook and line bluefishermen of the post war era that included Bert and Harold Stevens from Westbrook, the Chapman brothers and "Mouse" Gates from Groton, Ivan and Errol Crossman from Noank, Dick and Ann Hunter from New Haven, plus a few more whose names escape me.

Hooker came from the Connecticut River area, lived aboard his boat most of the summer and docked wherever he happened to be chasing the bluefish. He also worked alone, which was a good thing as his boat was a small raised foredeck lobster type of indeterminate age that could not have been more than 25 feet long. It was a rather clumsy, boxy looking boat that I suspect might have been home-built and was painted in a slap dash manner with a mix of dark grey and flat black, giving it a weird camouflaged appearance. Hooker was a tall, rangy guy with stringy coal black hair and arms that looked to be about four feet long. His normal attire on the grounds was a pair of huge hip boots (they must have been at least size 14) rolled all the way up and clipped to his belt, a tattered wool shirt with the sleeves cut off at the elbows, a dirty blue and white striped hat like the railroad engineers used to wear and a black rubber apron. He also usually hadn't shaved in several days.

In spite of his scarecrow-like appearance, Hooker was a pleasant fellow with a cheerful disposition and a crackerjack bluefisherman. I guess he had to have an easy going nature to live for weeks on end in a tiny cabin that could not have been more than eight feet long from the cabin bulkhead to the oak bitt, affording not more than crouching headroom for his 6 foot plus frame. He also shared his living quarters with the engine and some sort of stove whose stubby smokepipe projected from the starboard side of the foredeck. What the interior of the cabin looked like I never knew but, if it looked as scruffy as the outside, it must have made the *MAYFLOWER* look palatial.

With his exceptionally long arms, Hooker was a whiz at heaving and hauling and, having nobody else in the cockpit that he could snag with an errant jig, he would fling the fish aboard with such energy that sometimes they would go flying right back overboard on the other side. This didn't seem to worry him for he never had a temper tantrum like some other of the fishermen would do when this happened to them. Like many fishermen, he was paranoid that someone would steal what he considered to be a secret fishing spot. He could be Mohawking them every drift, and he would still move off the range if he saw a strange boat approaching.

He would then set-up well off to the side of the spot and go back to work, even though he knew right well that there was nothing there. If the stranger did not fall for this ruse and come over to where he was, he would tie a painted wooden replica of a bluefish to his jig and proceed to "catch" it every time down, hooting and hollering in feigned glee each time he landed the decoy. He would keep up this drill until either the stranger came over to his vicinity or it was plain that there was no use in persisting any longer in his charade. He would then come grudgingly back after wasting a lot of precious fishing time, claiming all the while that the other fisherman had probably stolen his range by getting a line on the spot with the binoculars before he, Hooker, had moved away.

One morning, although he had yelled over to us the night before that he would see us on the rip at daylight, Hooker didn't show up with the rest of the boats. While this was unusual, we were all busy trying to make a day's pay before the tide let go and it wasn't until the slack that my Dad commented, "I wonder where Hooker was this morning?" I shrugged it off and thought to myself that he probably was having trouble with the balky little Palmer gas engine which lived in his forecastle. This was not the case, for when we got home that afternoon, my Mom handed my Dad a copy of the Norwich Bulletin with an article about a fatal car accident in Salem the previous evening. It was Hooker all right. He and a unnamed passenger were coming from somewhere up the line in an old jalopy and one of his fishing boots had somehow become jammed between the accelerator and the brake pedal. The car had caromed off a tree on the left side of the twisting road, skidded across the highway and fetched up against a stone wall. The passenger escaped with only a few scratches, but poor old Hooker was dead on the spot. The paper identified him only as a Mr. Hooker, address unknown. I guess his boat must have been his only permanent address after all.

While I am reminiscing about captains I might as well record some nearly fatal accidents and rescues at sea among the charterboat fleet. Tony Faria, whose son Thomas founded the well-know tachometer firm, was another of the old timers who ran charters out of New London in the late 1940s. Tony's boat, at the time of this episode, was named *MY PAL* and, like our boat, was a semi-converted local lobsterboat type. This was later replaced by a new Downeast style boat called *MY PAL II* which, in turn, was renamed *LADY MARGARET* when it was purchased by Claude Adams Jr. The incident I am about to relate began on a nice May weekend while a group of about 15 charterboats and commercial handliners were trolling for pollock on the flood tide rips between Montauk Point and Great

Eastern Buoy. The fish, while not being completely uncooperative, were definitely not leaping into the boats. In local fisherman's parlance it would have been classified as a slow pick or even a slow desperate pick and, as usual, it dropped off to zero on the slack.

Just like the pre-start maneuvering prior to the start of a sailboat race, during slack water there was the usual milling around among the boats jockeying for position. The idea here was to be positioned properly so that you would be among the first to make a pass along the underwater ridge which would cause the tide rip to form as soon as the current increased. However, when the ebb made down, Gus Pitts ran the *MARIE* up ahead of the middle of Pollock Rip, threw the anchor over and slacked out enough warp to allow his stern to be just ahead of the first breaker. In a few minutes, first Ralph Pitts in the *MARGARET* and then Carl Darenberg in the *FORTENATE* followed suit. These actions effectively blocked off the rip for trolling and soon everyone was scrambling to get a spot as close to the presumed "hot" area as possible. We were anchored near the inshore end of the rip with Tony in the *MY PAL* about 6 or 8 boats offshore of us next to Frank Moss in *KUNO*.

With the full moon that week, the strong tides always associated with that lunar phase picked up very quickly, and soon we were really trolling at anchor rather than actually bottom fishing. It was a nice day for early May, but a chilly southeast wind had sprung up and there was a sizable rip running just astern of the row of anchored boats. Then it happened. There was a shout of alarm from the *MY PAL* as one of their passengers tumbled backwards over the port side into the 38 degree water and was swept rapidly astern into the rip. Someone aboard the boat alertly threw over a lifejacket that landed near enough to the man for him to paddle over and get a grip on it. However, he was a fairly large man to begin with and was wearing a heavy winter overcoat so, try as he might, he couldn't get more than one arm through the opening. Everybody up and down the line of boats was yelling at Tony to start his engine and go after him, but Tony was nowhere to be seen. Then it struck me, the *MY PAL* had one of the old type heavy-duty engines that started by hand, and I was certain that Tony was down below cranking it over as fast as he could, but no sounds were coming from the exhaust. In a few minutes, Tony came leaping out of the companionway door and hollered frantically that his engine wouldn't start and would somebody PLEASE go pick up the man.

By this time, the hapless customer had been carried down through 3 or 4 breakers that had swept completely over his head and it was plain to all that he was weakening fast and if somebody didn't pick him up very soon, it would be curtains. There was a flurry of activity in several of the boats near the *MY PAL* and, as we watched, Frank Moss got the *KUNO* started while his mate scrambled up on the bow and cut the anchor line with a knife. Frank cranked the wheel hard to port, slammed the throttle wide open, and with what looked like only a fraction of an inch to spare between the *KUNO* and the next boat, he spun her around and shot right through the first breaker. In less than a minute it was all over. The *KUNO* dove through the intervening combers at full speed until they reached the victim; the mate and a couple of the customers grabbed the man in the water and, with one concerted heave, dragged him over the rail and dumped him on the deck. Frank then turned around and idled up through the rip until he reached the smooth water in front of the first breaker, slid alongside the *MY PAL* and the guy just stepped back aboard, apparently none the worse for wear after nearly losing his life. You would expect the episode to have put a damper on Tony's charter but, inside of 5 minutes, the swimmer was back on deck in a borrowed set of foul weather gear laughing and joking with the others. Nevertheless, you can be sure that, from our standpoint, after we had witnessed what could easily have been a fatal accident, we always watched our customers a lot more carefully when we were anchored in a strong current.

Another extremely daring rescue took place in the Race one fall morning in the 1950s, among our own local group. It is only fair to admit at the outset that it is absolutely beyond question that none of us should have been there, period. Even with the invaluable assistance of more than 40 years of hindsight, the reasons all of us were fishing under conditions extremely hazardous to life and property are far from clear. They were, I assume, related to a combination of stupidity, greed and peer pressure, as well as not wanting to be the first captain to give it up and head home. It was simply much too rough in the Race that day for any of us to be there trying to catch a few bluefish.

We were in the second day of an unusually persistent southeasterly gale, which is an abnormal condition. Most of our coastal storms start out as northeasters and, after the low moves by, shift fairly quickly into the northerly or the southwesterly quadrant before dying away. There must have been very bad weather offshore for, in addition to the huge ebb tide rip you would expect to be pushed up by a southeast gale, there was a big groundswell rolling through compounding the situation. This unusual combination of conditions only occurs in the Race once or twice every 10 years and until you have seen what can happen, you are likely to fish too close to the rip and be caught napping. On this particular day, several of the captains who, like my Dad, had spent time fishing at Montauk Point where this sea state occurs more often, knew from past experience the dangers inherent under the present conditions and stayed at least 100 yards ahead of the rip. My Dad had mentioned the possibility of rogue (unusually high and dangerous) waves during the radio chit chat that goes on continually between the captains but, as none had occurred, many boats were fishing closer to the rip than he felt was prudent.

The group of charterboats were fishing between what used to be called the "Tower and Light Range" and the deep water to the south towards Little Gull. The sky was black with birds and the water just ahead of the rip was alive with breaking bluefish. A few of the boats, Joe Wilk in the *POSEIDON* and Paul Marcella in the *GIPSY* among them, were right in the thick of things down there near the rip and were catching well. We were up ahead of them about 75 yards or so and, while we were picking away, they were obviously out-catching us by at least three to one. I mentioned this several times to my Dad and he finally got tired of hearing about it, for he told me to knock it off as he considered it to be just too dangerous that close to the rip. I was far from convinced, but I knew from the tone of his voice I had pushed the subject to the limit and I had better button my lip.

Every now and then a larger than normal breaker would form and roll ominously out of the rip, making the boats in what my Old Man called the *Danger Zone* crank on the power and run ahead almost up to where we were fishing in order to keep the sea from breaking over their transoms. It was plain to me that my Dad was becoming increasingly unhappy about the sea conditions. After we had to steam ahead to get out of the way of the boats behind us, which were running away from one of the bigger waves, he announced we were going to wrap it up and head home before we got run down. Half of our charter had been seasick most of the day, and those who were still up and around were cold, wet and probably on the edge of succumbing, so there was no objection from them either. In a few minutes we were underway to the northwest, both to get a good angle on the seas before turning to the northeast towards North Dumpling, as well as to gain enough distance to keep from being carried down into the tide rips in the deep water between Valiant Rock and the lee of Fishers Island.

We had steamed just about far enough ahead of the rip to make our turn to the northeast when my Dad startled us all by shouting, "Wow, look at that big one coming out of the rip back of us! That's just what I was afraid of and if those guys are still back near the rip it's going to eat them alive before they can get out of the way." Wow was right! There was a towering wall of water that looked more than two stories high marching swiftly out of the face of the rip. From our vantage point a half mile away, it dwarfed the boats in its path and it was obvious that it was quickly overtaking their efforts to escape up the tide to safety. As it reached the shoaler water up ahead of the rip, the smooth, nearly vertical face of the wave reacted to the pull of the bottom and, just as on the north coast of Hawaii, the wave began to tumble over and break in a crescendo of foam that completely engulfed the boats in its path.

We could do nothing at our distance and, even if we were there, it was an open question if we would have endangered our lives and those of our passengers to give assistance. In another moment the wave had spent its energy and, although we could see that all of the boats were still afloat, two of them were milling around in circles. Then, while we watched in disbelief, both of them turned to the southeast and slowly went into the huge rip bow first. There didn't seem to be a snowball's chance in Hell that either of them would be able to survive in that sea, and we were all at a loss to explain why they had seemingly attempted suicide in that manner. I was almost frantic with worry and asked my Dad if we were going to do anything. He nodded in assent and said, "Yup, we're going to keep on heading toward home. They're either going to be OK or they're not. Anyway, we're to far away to be of any help and, even if we were there, I doubt if I would take a chance of adding any more casualties to the list by risking your lives."

There was a buzz of talk among the captains over the radio and although a number of frantic calls were made to the boats who had gone into the rip, there was no immediate reply. The two whose actions had seemed so outrageously dangerous turned out to be *GIPSY* and the *POSEIDON* and in a few more minutes we were all overjoyed to hear Paul Marcella's calm voice come over the radio. "Hey POSEI-DON" and Joe's laconic reply, "Yeah, go ahead Paul." "Thanks a lot Joe." "That's OK Goomba, don't see that I had any choice but to take the chance." "Well, thanks anyway Joe. By the way, what do you suppose is the best way to get back out through the rip?" By this time everyone was asking them what had happened, but the only information Joe would give was his standard reply when he didn't want to give any info over the radio. "I'll see you on the dock, Cappy."

Later on, the whole story came out, for it is virtually impossible to keep anything secret between charter captains for very long. The story was simply this. When the huge comber crashed right over the *GIPSY*, two of Paul's people, one of which was his son Jim, had been washed overboard and, by the time Paul was able to get the boat back under control, they were a considerable distance astern. The reason they were so far behind was because the force of the breaking sea on the transom, assisted by the fact that the boat was already at top speed trying to outrun the wave, caused it to surf ahead for over a hundred yards beyond the two men struggling in the water. Joe was horrified to see Paul turning around but, looking back, immediately realized what had taken place and also recognized that Paul would only have time to rescue one of the men before the other would be carried into the rip by the swift current and almost certainly drowned in the huge breaking waves. Without hesitation, Joe turned around to help and between them they managed to pick up both men in the nick of time; but not in time to keep the boats from being swept into the rip by the current. Once they had entered the breakers there was no choice but to keep both boats headed slowly into the seas until the size of the waves decreased enough so they could turn around without being in danger of getting rolled over. As it turned out, Paul rescued the customer and Joe picked up Paul's son Jim, both cold and wet, but thankfully, alive and well.

On another bad day in the Race, my Dad and I very nearly became a statistic while the two of us were commercial handlining for bluefish. We had followed a bunch of fish down into the rip at the setting of the ebb and, when they quit biting, were headed up the tide trying to get out of what had turned into a dangerously large rip. We were just coming out of the first breaker when the rudder came out of the water as we went over the crest, the boat slewed around to port and literally fell off the front edge of the breaker broadside into the trough. I thought we were a goner for sure. My Dad, who was steering from the flybridge, yelled, "HANG ON BF." He let go of the steering wheel (the only time I ever saw him do that) and wrapped his arms around the mast. I grabbed the port bitt with both hands and wrapped my legs around the tiller, which was hard over to port in an attempt to turn the boat to starboard. We hit with a crash and buried the starboard side of the boat almost to amidships. The mast was lying in the water and my Dad was nearly submerged. We lay there on our beam ends for what seemed like an eternity. As I watched the next breaker come rushing down, it looked as if it would finish us off. Fortunately, most of it broke on our keel and, instead of sending us to the bottom, it acted as a lever to straighten the boat back onto her feet, and we lived to fish another day.

My brother John participated in a different type of rescue when he took my place aboard the *ANNA R* one day, so that I could go to the Eastern States Exposition with my wife. My Dad had fished until dark and they were heading home when he saw two or three boats and a lot of flashing lights to the west of Race Rock. Something was obviously very wrong, and he took a swing over to see what was going on. When they got close to one of the boats, the skipper screamed over that they had lost a man overboard and could not locate him in the dark and PLEASE help them find him. My Dad shut the motor off so he could hear any cries for help and, when he did this, they could hear someone on a boat nearby shouting, "Over Here, Over Here!" They steamed right over and discovered that a lobsterman, who was alone in his boat, had found the man floating unconscious in the water, but was unable to haul him aboard alone as the guy weighed well over 250 lbs. The lobsterman was lying over the rail on his stomach, desperately trying to hang onto the man and keep his head out of the water as the boat slatted back and forth furiously in the steep chop. My Dad sent John to the bow and, when they got close alongside, John was able to leap over onto the other boat. He dashed aft and, between the two of them, they managed to drag the man into the cockpit. They then headed for the Coast Guard station in Silver Eel Pond at Fishers Island at full speed. The guy wasn't breathing at all, and John said later he was sure that the poor fellow was going to be dead on arrival. Nevertheless, he rolled him over and began the prone pressure technique of artificial resuscitation he had learned as a Boy Scout. In a few minutes, the man gave a groan, threw up a mess of seawater and took the first of several shuddering breaths. By the time they got to the Coast Guard station he was breathing regularly but, as a precaution, the Coast Guard crewmen took him to the Lawrence and Memorial Hospitals in their patrol boat for observation. One final note: the guy never even called or sent a post card of thanks to John or the lobsterman for saving his life. So much for gratitude.

Rogue wave in the Race on an otherwise only sloppy sea state, 1960s.

I rescued the lone man aboard just before the boat sank, mid 1960s.

John E. (Jack) Wilbur, Master Mariner.

Chapter Twenty

SOME HARD TIMES AND A TRIBUTE TO JACK WILBUR

In putting together this group of recollections about growing up in Noank and going fishing for a living, I would be remiss if I didn't include the following events which were very important factors in my life and I want to make sure they do not go unrecorded. The first paragraphs use the building of my 40 foot wooden boat to set the stage for an episode, and a belated public recognition, involving one of Noank's premier seamen in this or any previous age.

About a year before my Dad was diagnosed as having bone cancer, the two of us had come to the reluctant conclusion that the prospects for making a decent living in our 31 foot handliner/dragger/charterboat were very likely going to decrease in the next 10 years. Boy, were we ever correct. In my Dad's opinion, unless we were prepared to spend more than $100,000.00 for a proper dragger over 50 feet in length, we would be better off financially by concentrating on charterboat fishing and harpoon swordfishing. If we were going to shift our emphasis toward recreational fishing, it was also plain that the 8 knot, gasoline powered Webb Eldridge hull we were using would soon be too small and much too slow to compete effectively in that trade. Both he and I had been very impressed with some of the boats Walter McInness had designed and it was decided to engage him to draw up a set of plans for us when we wrapped up the 1957 season in November. Unfortunately, during the summer my Dad's leg began to bother him a lot. By Thanksgiving the problem was diagnosed as bone cancer and his leg was amputated above the knee.

This naturally put a hold on our plans for a new boat, but his recovery was remarkably swift and he was back running the boat by spring. By the start of the second season following his amputation, the doctors could find no indication that his cancer had spread, so Bob Whittaker and I went up to McInness's office in Boston and settled on a design for the new hull. My Dad seemed very pleased with our choice but shortly after we had made this step, two problems arose which cast doubt on the wisdom of the project. First of all, Webb Eldridge's widow, Clara, sold the boatyard to Bob Hellier and, even more importantly, my Dad's health took a serious turn for the worse. The first hurdle was easily overcome by my leasing the boatshop from Bob Hellier, but my Dad's problem proved to be unsolvable. He and I talked the situation over and it was decided to proceed regardless of his deteriorating health. My Dad was one tough minded individual, for in spite of knowing full well he was terminally ill, he was intensely interested in the project and had me spend some time with him every evening bringing him up to date on our progress. As Bob and I framed and planked it, I took pictures of the hull to help illustrate our progress for my Dad, but he died before it was half completed.

My memories of the next two years are actually rather blurred from overwork and lack of sleep. Between charter fishing summers, most of the time without a deckhand to save money, running Earle Wadsworth's HIRAM over and back to Fishers Island 2 trips a day in the winter, and trying to complete a 40 foot wooden sportfisherman under the guiding hand of Bob Whittaker, I seldom got more than 4 hours of sleep a night. My normal winter schedule went something like this: rise at 5:00 A.M.; get breakfast; drive my brother John's 1931 Model A Ford rumble-seat coupe to Stonington; crank up the Mack diesel on the HIRAM and ferry Remington Rand's instructors to Fishers Island; dead-head back to Stonington; drive to the boatshop and work on the boat till 3:00 P.M.; drive back to Stonington; chug over to Fishers Island and return to Stonington with the instructors; drive home and gulp down a hot meal; then go back to the boatshop until 12:30 to 1:30 A.M.; drive home and collapse in bed until 5:00 A.M. when the cycle began again.

It was a killing schedule, but I was only 30 years old, had plenty of incentive and, most importantly, had the strength of desperation, for we were in debt over our heads and then some. By the spring of the second year, the boat was almost completed, but we were dead, flat, stony broke and owed everybody we had

Hauling ANNA R III *out of Eldridge Boatyard shed, 1959.*

done business with. We were rescued from the brink of disaster by an 11th hour personal loan from Jack Wilbur or we would have lost both the boat and our home as well. Jack literally saved my family from financial ruin, for I had spent our meager savings, emptied our children's bank accounts and exhausted every dollar of credit the banks would extend to me. I simply didn't have a clue where to turn. On the day he extended a totally unsolicited helping hand to me, the boat was still perched in the boatyard unlaunched, and I was sitting dejectedly on the rail trying to figure out what to do next when Jack climbed up the ladder and stepped on deck. After the usual greetings, he casually asked me how things were going, and when I replied that things were going lousy and I was stuck, he pressed me for details. I told him I needed about another $4,000.00 to put the boat in service, but the banks had shut me off as a poor credit risk because I was way behind in paying even the interest on the loans I had taken out to build the boat.

Jack stood there for a few minutes and then said in an off-hand conversational manner, "Are you sure you need only another $4,000.00 to finish the boat?" I replied in the affirmative. Jack nodded, more to himself than to me, and shifted the conversation to another topic. We chatted for awhile and then Jack said he had to get going, climbed back down the ladder and off he went. In less than 10 minutes he was back with a personal check made out for $4,500.00 and handed it to me. I didn't know what to say and was stammering away trying to express my gratitude for the unsolicited loan. Jack, as always, was unperturbed and told me to calm down and get back to work on the boat. "I'm leaving on a trip around the world for American Export Lines in a couple of days and won't be back for three or four months at the earliest," he said. "This deal is between you and me and nobody else. If I come home safe, you owe me 4,500 dollars. If something goes wrong and I don't come home it's yours. In either case, I want you to promise to keep your mouth shut about it." Needless to say, I finished the boat, Jack came home safely and I managed to pay him back before the year was out. It has been over 35 years since this took place and Jack is no longer with us. After all these years, I have decided that my pledge to keep my mouth shut about his generosity has run out. It's high time to make his good deed public as a belated tribute to Jack and as an example of the best side of human nature.

Launching day ANNA R III, 1960. Rosalie, Robert, Beth Ann, "Samuel Beauregard", I'm at helm.

Dad about 1950.

Chapter Twenty-One

A BRIEF RECOUNTING
OF MY DAD'S CHILDHOOD

Originally not planned for publication, this chapter incorporates a major part of what little I know of my Dad's early years in Noank, plus a practical joke in which he participated. Because this aspect of our family will probably be lost forever if I exclude it, and I think it may illustrate how a really disadvantaged childhood does not keep one from growing up into a responsible citizen, here it is.

My Dad, in his early adolescence, would be considered by any current social worker worth his or her salt to be a seriously underprivileged and definitely rebellious youth. As near as I can determine, even as a child, his mother and he never got along well and in 1909, when he was 13 years old, his father, age 40, died after a prolonged illness which appears to have been an undiagnosed case of tuberculosis.His mother, Edna, very soon remarried and prepared to move to Flagstaff, Arizona with her new husband. So far, no big deal, right? Wrong! For reasons I never could get him to explain in any detail, my Dad and his new stepfather, Homer See, just didn't get along at all. From some hints which slipped out over the years, I expect a great part of the problem was probably due to Homer being a strict disciplinarian of the SPARE THE ROD AND SPOIL THE CHILD school of parenting. My Dad being, as I have indicated, more than a little rebellious (he always considered this aspect of his character as being strong-minded), made no bones about his dislike of his stepfather and just flatly refused to move to Arizona with them. How, you may ask, could a youth of 13 refuse to accompany his family to Arizona and make it stick. After all, they could have bundled him aboard the train with them and it would be case closed. This was, in fact, exactly what they informed him they were going to do, whether he approved of the move or not. It was a good try on their part, but it just didn't work.

Although we worked together on a small fishing boat for 16 years and had many long discussions on a vast array of subjects that ranged from politics to premartial sex, he was extremely reticent when the topic of his childhood and formative years came up. It's quite possible he simply didn't want me to get any

157

wild ideas about being too independent for my own good, but he would never go into any great detail about this period in his life. The only answer I got when I asked him how he managed to talk his mother into leaving him behind, was that he told her the following: "Sure, you can force me to go to Arizona with you, but the trains run in both directions, and as soon as I can get away from you, I'll hop the next freight train back to Noank." He must have convinced them that hopping a freight and riding the rails back across the continent was not just an idle threat, for they eventually took off without him and, other than sporadic letters between my Mom and my maternal grandmother after she married my Dad, they didn't see each other for about 30 years.

His plan to get home in a freight car was not as far fetched as it might appear to us today. In the early part of this century there was an entire sub-culture of men, called Hoboes or Tramps, who roamed all over the country by hitching rides on freight trains. Just about any medium sized town served by rail would have a cluster of these men living in small camps along the railroad right of way in what were called "Hobo Jungles." Even as late as the 1940s, we would often look down from the railroad overpass and see men riding in one of the open gondolas or hiding on flat cars between the freight.

At any rate, his mother must have realized that it was far better to leave him in a known location, than to not know where he was at all. Although my Dad was very vague when he talked about where he lived after his mother left, he apparently moved in with his grandparents, William Gadson (Bill Gad) Rathbun and Lavina Baker Rathbun, until they passed away within a few months of each other in 1913. Then, for a time, he lived with Augustus V. Morgan who, either the courts or his mother had designated as his guardian. Some time after this, when Dad's cousin Helen Rathbun married Halstead Brown, he moved back to the Rathbun homestead on Church Street. Why he hadn't become a juvenile delinquent by then, I'll never figure out, but I do know that he always gave his grandmother Lavina Rathbun a lot of credit for helping him stay within striking distance of the straight and narrow. He also had another role model in his grandfather "Bill Gad" Rathbun. According to his tombstone in Noank Valley Cemetery, Bill Gad's own father, Benjamin Franklin Rathbun (my namesake) had died at sea on the way home from Jamaica when Bill Gad was only one year old. His mother never remarried and young Bill Gad must have been a difficult child to raise without a husband, for he was not yet a teenager when he ran away to sea on a sailing ship bound for California. What he did for a living while he was away was always a matter of intense local speculation. All I know for sure is that he returned after quite a few years and bought a fishing schooner, so he must have done all right at something.

A lucky break that may have given my Dad the push he needed to set him on the right path took place when Mr. William I. Spicer, whose home on Spicer Avenue now houses the Town of Groton Recreation Department, sent his son to Suffield Academy. By all accounts, the Spicer youngster was inclined to be more than a little wild, and his father, who was at that time Noank's richest man, sent some of the local boys, including my father, to Suffield Academy to get both an education and to keep a close eye on his son. Although I don't know who else's education was fully paid by Mr. Spicer, my Dad was accompanied by Albert (Bert) Patterson, Nelson C.L.(Bud) Brown Sr., Wilfred (Hoot) Ellis and Dr. E. Roland Hill. The boys all did well there with Bert Patterson and Hoot Ellis excelling in sports, Bud Brown in music and my Dad becoming president of his senior class; a fact I was totally unaware of until Nelson C.L. Brown Jr. gave me a copy of the 1916 Suffield Academy Year Book several years ago.

Benjamin F. Rathbun Sr. Suffield Academy Year Book, 1916.

After graduation he was inducted into the Army, which sent him to Carnegie Institute to study radio. After the Armistice was signed in 1918 there were no jobs available in Pennsylvania for a partially trained radio technician and he returned to Noank looking for work. The only job he could get was as a sternman on John Daboll's lobsterboat. Although his sights had been set on working in radio as a career, by the end of the first summer he was hooked, and he remained a fisherman all the rest of his life.

At the beginning, I mentioned I would tell of a practical joke my Dad told me about, in which he and some other Noank youths were involved. But first a little local history for background. During the beginning of the 20th century, the Palmer Shipyard was still in its heyday and employed a considerable number of workers who were not native to the area. A portion of this influx of outsiders were housed in the rooming houses and tenements which once graced the village and, with only cisterns and shallow wells supplying water, many of these places had limited facilities for washing clothes, especially for a single man. A short news item in the Noank News column of the January 16, 1899 New London Day recorded how this void in amenities was first filled. "Our first and only resident Chinese laundryman, George Hung Chung is supplying a long-felt want." George Hung Chung set up his business in the building which now contains the Corner Closet Shop, Beauty Parlor and Pratt-Wright Galleries. He apparently prospered for many years. A Chinese laundryman would not have been newsworthy in New York, but in turn-of-the-century Noank it was certainly unusual. In keeping with the general tendency of youths to pick on anyone perceived to be different and somewhat vulnerable, the young men of the village were always trying to pull off a prank on the Chinaman. None of the kids messed with another "different" man known as John the Devil for, in addition to his swarthy complexion and wild appearance, the story (actually totally untrue) going around among the youths was that he was on the lam from some fatally violent episode. In contrast, the Chink, as they called him, was a slightly built, meek looking man who minded his own business and was therefore a safe target for their horseplay.

Their most notable episode came when word got out that the Chink was suffering from some kind of intestinal illness. A group of the local youths were hanging around, trying to decide what to do next, when somebody said he heard the Chink was suffering from a Bilious Attack. When I was growing up, my Dad often complained about having one of these, but it must not be a common ailment today, as I haven't heard the term used for many years. Possibly medical science has wiped it out, along with Sluggish Liver and Feminine Weakness, both formerly very popular illnesses. This must be what took place, for if they were still maladies suffered by large numbers of Americans, there would certainly be a multinational drug company running television ads for pills that were reputed to cure them. A second legitimate reason for the absence of Bilious Attacks in the index of diseases listed in my Home Medical Advisor is possibly because there may be more profit in curing Headaches, PMS and Depression, all currently very popular illnesses. Furthermore, even the medical magazines that we often read with great trepidation in doctors' waiting rooms, fail to mention it, although they do tell us much more than most of us ever wanted to know about some of the more exotic diseases known to mankind such as Ebola and Lassa Fever. Anyway, information that the poor oriental was sick brought up the potential for a practical joke the group might be able to pull off at the expense of the gullible laundryman. After some thought, they decided to pool their meager funds and buy him some medicine whose effects would not actually harm him but would, hopefully, really cause him to worry.

Today we are so used to the requirements for FDA approval and truth in advertising for drugs that we often forget that, in the early part of this century, just about any type of medicine was available over the counter for the asking. The old warning of "Let the buyer beware" was a known fact of life to everybody. If what you had just bought didn't help or even harmed you grievously, it was just your tough luck. What specific medical concoction the guys purchased from Dr. Hill is now uncertain, but they managed to convince the object of their prank that it would quickly cure his intestinal troubles and advised him to drink the whole bottle at once. The patent medicine which they gave him was known to cause the tongue and the urine to turn a bright green and was obviously not a poison or the tale would have had a tragic ending

Later in the day, the gang went back to see how the Chink was making out. He didn't come to the counter when they entered the store but, by listening closely, muffled chanting could be heard coming from the back room where the living quarters were. Nothing daunted, they all just kept on going and trooped through the rear door into his small apartment. There they found their unsuspecting victim seated on a stool in front of a cracked mirror, chanting quietly in what they figured must have been Chinese. He had changed from the black pants and white open-necked shirt he usually wore while working into a red embroidered silk robe and was slowly combing out his long coal black hair with a large ivory comb. "What's up?" somebody said. The oriental kept on chanting for a few more minutes, until he came to what sounded like the end of whatever incantation he was intoning. He looked at the motley group gathered around his stool and said calmly "Tongue gleen, piss gleen, bout half hour make die." He turned back toward the mirror, picked up the comb, began to chant again and went back to combing his hair. Nobody could figure out what to say at this development, so they all just drifted back out through the store and left the poor fellow to find out for himself that he was going to live after all.

My wife, Rosalie, and me, 1950.

CONNECTIONS & EPILOGUE

I think it would be quite safe to say that to most of us who have had the good fortune to grow up in Noank and continued to live here all their adult life, our village is a truly special place. While I cannot pretend to speak for anyone other than myself, my feeling of connectedness to Noank and its lifestyle is related, in some undefinable way, to the sea. Upon reflection, this ought not to be a surprise, for Noank's fortunes were closely tied to marine activities even before English settlers arrived in Connecticut and began to elbow the Pequots out of their ancestral summer fishing camps. The relationship of Noankers to fishing and other forms of marine commerce has remained strong throughout the intervening centuries. This, in turn, has attracted men and women of like mind to reside here and contribute to the unique spirit of the community. This continued connection with its seafaring heritage may be at the core of the cohesiveness within the village which has allowed Noank to remain, at least up to now, much more independent than most of the other villages in the area.

To elaborate, I am thoroughly convinced we are all connected to those who preceded us in time and space. If my unconventional world view concerning the presence of a true "community spirit" is someday found to have a factual basis, I will not be at all shocked. In this supposedly enlightened age, we tend to scoff at the so-called heathen religious views of the Native Americans. Nevertheless, an unprejudiced peek into Noank's past will show I am not alone in my conjecture. Even though the historical accounts were written with a strong bias toward colonial expansion, it is clear that during the 1712 forced relocation of the remainder of the Pequots from Noank to Mashantucket, the Indians firmly believed the spirits of their ancestors pervaded Noank. Whether my feeling concerning the presence of a unique Noank "spirit" is justified or merely the end result of the collected influence of like oriented people over a very long time is, of course, beyond our ability to discern. But, whatever the cause, I find it attractive to believe there may be more than happenstance to the fact that the chief of the newly resurgent Pequots has chosen Noank as his new home.

At any rate, for more than 100 years, Noank has been the home of my direct male ancestors, with over 80 relatives now buried in its cemetery, so it is not unusual to feel a strong attachment and an underlying connection to the place which defies our conventional view of reality. This subconscious feeling of connectedness to those who preceded us in Noank was undoubtedly fortified by my very close association with my Dad. When you spend 16 years of your youth on a 32 foot boat working for an extremely competent skipper with a strong sense of history, who is also your father, you tend to unconsciously begin to act and think much like him in spite of yourself. His way of looking at the world has had a major influence on my life in ways I never would have believed possible when I was younger. Although not originally my goal in recording a few of the noteworthy happenings from those years, these reminiscences about my life are an attempt to pass on a few of my Dad's views and acknowledge his profound influence on me which I was not mature enough to recognize while he was alive.

All in all, I have few regrets for my decision to go fishing out of Noank. Even if I were given the chance to do it over, I don't think I would trade the nearly 50 years I spent making my principal living off the water for any other career choice. Speaking of careers, I'm not sure I actually had what would nowadays be considered a career, unless it was as a Jack of All Trades. This last spring, when I was revising my resume, I realized that, at one time or another, I have supported myself and my family by a pretty extensive list of marine and land-based trades. At the risk of being boring, it includes: lobstering; dragging; handlining for groundfish, bluefish, sea bass and tuna; tub trawling for cod; bay scalloping; harpoon swordfishing; owning and operating both fishing and sailing charterboats; delivering yachts up and down the Atlantic coast; sportfishing out of Eleuthera; working for Cross Sound Ferry; and operating a marine surveying business. In addition to these water-related professions, I worked ashore during the winter months for building contractors Harrell Brown, Bob Goodman and Jack Fleishman. I helped build between 15 and 20 new homes and remodeled innumerable others. I worked at Mystic Shipyard as a yacht painter and at Noank Shipyard as a boat repairer. With the invaluable direction and assistance of Bob Whittaker, during 1959 and 1960, I build the 39 ft wooden sportfisherman I spoke of in the tribute to Jack Wilbur. In 1973, in a little over 4 months, I built the present *ANNA R IV*, starting from a bare hull. She is a 42 foot fiberglass sportfisherman which I used for almost 18 years before turning her over to my son Franklin. As I said one time when I was introducing myself to the Maine/New Hampshire Sea Grant Directors, my PHD is in generalities.

Looking back over the last 50 odd years, I realize full well that the opportunity I had to participate in a great many fisheries, both commercial and sportfishing, will probably not be available to those who are growing up today. As we have progressed from the Joshua Slocum methods of navigation to the era of the GPS and the World Wide Web, we have also managed to overfish many, if not most, of the desirable marine species on which we depended. Not only that, participation in the commercial harvest is no longer open to anyone who wants to go fishing. Both commercial fishing boats and many species of fish are already heavily regulated and restricted, almost 10,000 square miles of the most productive grounds are presently closed and severe reductions in allowable days are already being implemented. Unfortunately, this change from the traditional unrestricted access to fish when, where and how you chose is probably as permanent as the one which took place during my Dad's lifetime when internal combustion engines replaced sail and that way of life was over forever. These are sobering thoughts, but life goes on as it always has and I have confidence that those Noankers who follow my generation will continue to be influenced by the unique spirit of this place and adapt to the new conditions as readily as those who preceded them in Noank, which I consider to be one of the nicest places on the planet.

ANNA R IV *(fiberglass) and me, 1972.*

Me, son Franklin, grandson Jeremy, 1996.

The author in front of his home at Riverview Avenue, Noank, 1995.

GLOSSARY

Abigail's Island: A small round island in the Mystic River adjacent to Mystic River Marina.

Ahoy Island: The name Arthur Henry (who lived in the house once built on Quirk Island) bestowed on the island to the northeast of Quirk.

Alice L. Pendleton: The 4-masted schooner formerly grounded and deteriorating where Noank Shipyard's south dock is now located. Brought to Noank near the end of Prohibition in order to be refitted as a mother-ship for the rum-runners which then smuggled the liquor ashore. The Volstead Act (Prohibition) was repealed before she was ready and she was abandoned. She eventually sank and the hulk was a favorite, albeit usually out-of-bounds playground for Noank youths.

Anabaptist: Religious sect founded in Switzerland c. 1522 which denied the validity of infant baptism and practiced baptism of adults by immersion. In the 1600s, they were often persecuted and even expelled by the Puritans of the Massachusetts Bay Colony. Present day Baptists are among their direct descendants.

Anchor Warp: Anchor line or rope.

Anderson, Robert P. Sr.: U.S. Circuit Court Judge, Father of Robert P.(Chip) Anderson Jr. and one of my Dad's lifelong friends.

B.F.: My nickname when a youth and what my Dad always called me.

Bitt: Square or round posts used to secure mooring or anchor lines.

Black Diamond: A brand of commercial grade foul weather gear, formerly the premier type favored by fishermen.

Brown, Halstead: My Dad's second cousin by marriage. He lived on Church Street in the house now owned by Lavinia Wilbur, nee Coon. His wife, Helen, and Raymond Coon's wife, Esther, were sisters.

Cat Boat: A broad beamed sailboat type characterized by a single unstayed mast near the bow and a large outboard rudder; inevitably gaff rigged.

Cholera Bank: Formerly very productive fishing ground about 20 miles southeast of New York Harbor.

Cod End: The small end of a funnel-shaped beam or otter trawl in which the fish collect. Made of heavy twine and protected against chafing.

Collins Hill: Old local name for Brook Street from the Memorial to the top of the hill.

Coon, Raymond: Husband of Esther (Rathbun) Coon and father of Lavinia Wilbur. He had a fish-market on town dock prior to 38 hurricane. Later, he ran the gas station (now the Noank Service Center) across Ward Avenue from the old Noank Grammar School (now Noank Park).

Crossman, Ivan: Father of Errol and Arnold Crossman and my Dad's best friend.
The builder, with Bob Whittaker, of the 32 ft. lobsterboat *FALCON*.

Cuthbert, Alex: Lived in my house during the 1930s. Became keeper of an estate on Masons Island and was skipper of the *MADELYNE*, built by Bob Whittaker.

Davis, Mel: Worked at EB and lived in my house from about 1943 until 1950. We had no car at that time and my Dad normally rode to work with him.

Doubleday, Abner: Inventor of the sport of Baseball.

Douglas, Harry: Charterboat fisherman. Lived in Dunn's house on Pearl Street.

Eldridge, Grover: Owned and operated the *Reliance* and the *Black Hawk*, Noank's last two commercial fishing schooners employing dories. Primarily fished for tilefish using hand-hauled tub trawls. Lived in the house at the foot of Wilbur Court.

Ellis, Lauren: Commercial fisherman; skipper of the *IDELLA*. Lived in Eva Wright's house on Main Street. His son Walter blinded Donald Clark in a gunning accident and they moved to California shortly afterwards.

Fish Packing House: Generally, a facility connected to a dock used for unloading fish from boats. Normally included an insulated room for storage of block ice, an ice grinding machine, storage facilities for barreled or boxed fish awaiting shipment to markets, plus an area for empty barrels and boxes.

Focsle: A colloquial contraction of forecastle. Located below decks in the forward portion of a vessel and normally used for crew accommodations.

Ford, Albert (Bert): Uncle of Orion Ford of Ford's Lobsters.

Foresail: Although also used in square-riggers, in this instance the sail attached to the forward mast of a schooner.

Fort H.G. Wright: The now decommissioned fort located at the western end of Fishers Island. Built during the Spanish-American war and manned until the 1950s.

Fulton Market: Famous New York City wholesale fish market.

G-Men: (Government Men) Formerly a common term for the FBI.

Georges Bank: Offshore fishing ground east of Cape Cod. Formerly referred to as the "Winter Fishing Grounds" by Gloucester schooner-men.

Gravesend Bay: Bay in S. Brooklyn on the east side of New York City's Upper Bay.

Ground Cables: Lines, formerly rope but now steel, running between the paravanes (trawl doors) and the otter trawl opening. Originally quite short but now sometimes 600 to 900 feet in length.

Hadley, Charles: Commercial fisherman on Noank schooners. The vessel he was working aboard was sunk by gunfire from a German submarine during WW-1 after the German captain had allowed the crew to abandon ship in their dories.

Headfast: Also referred to as a Stakefast. Colloquially, a heavy manila cable used to tie boats to the oak stakes which formerly lined the southeast side of the Mystic River channel and were scattered throughout West Cove.

Henry, Arthur: Claimed and named Quirk Island in the late 1800s. Lived there, with 2 single girls, for several summers in a cottage he had a Noank carpenter build. Theodore Driesor was a close friend and frequent visitor to the island. Henry's book, *An Island Cabin*, published in 1902, is long out of print. There is a copy at the Noank Historical Society Museum.

Hewitt, Elmer: Father of author George Hewitt.

Highliner: A top producing commercial fisherman. Probably the most prestigious accolade in that field.

Hill, Dr. E. Roland: Son of Noank's famous Dr. Hill and friend of my Dad. Practiced in Mystic. His wife was sister of real estate agent "Bud" Wallace LeRoy.

Iron (or Ironing): Colloquial term for harpooning a swordfish.

J.A.: My brother John Alan's nickname when a youth and what my Dad almost always called him.

Jones, Miss Edna: Lived at 66 Riverview Avenue. Now the home of John Rathbun.

Laffargue, Gerard: Father of Noankers George, Gerard and Robert Laffargue, Helen Carpenter and Blanche Kayrukstis.

Langworthy, Maxson(Max): Lived on Potter Court. Ran a 31 ft. Webb Eldridge charterboat out of Fishers Island up to WW-2. His father was Captain Henry Langworthy, one of Noank's highliner schooner skippers. Two of Henry's most noteworthy commands were the schooners *Benjamin W. Latham* and *Tartar*.

Lathrop Engine Company: Founded by Walter Lathrop in the early 1900s and, up until the 1950s, one of the leading builders of marine gasoline engines in America. For additional information see "Memories of a Small Town Mechanic" by Edward Welles published by the Groton Public Library.

Lazy Line: In a side trawler, the rope running from a trawl door to the upper portion of the cod end. Used to pull the cod end alongside to allow the body of the net to be more easily retrieved. With the almost universal change to stern trawlers and net reels, it is now seldom used.

Longlining: Generally, a floating variation of a groundfish tub, or hook, trawl used beyond the continental shelf to catch oceanic species such as swordfish and the tunas. The most striking features are the length of the main line, which can be as much as 30 to 40 MILES and the placement of the branch lines (called gangions in a bottomfish trawl) which are sometimes hundreds of yards apart.

MacDonald, Arthur(Artie) Commercial fisherman and brother to Walter MacDonald.

MacDonald, Eugene(Gene): Had a two-story hardware store on Front Street about where Juanita Haines' house is today. At one time, the upper story was used as the meeting place of "The American Mechanics" fraternal order, but when they departed, the hardware store overflowed into their area. Gene's store was stocked with an incredible assortment of hardware and general merchandise piled in every nook and cranny. Slow moving stock was likely to be anywhere, upstairs or down, and even Gene often had only a general idea where a specific item was located. If he was busy, and you had time to spare, he would point out the general area in which he felt the item might be found, and then turn you loose to find it, if you could.

Make and Break: Old style, heavy duty, 2-cycle gasoline engine. Used a different ignition technique and seldom had a reverse gear. The engine was reversed by stopping it at top-dead-center and then starting it in the opposite rotation, a very tricky maneuver requiring practice to avoid crashing into things.

Manila Marline: Two-stranded manila cordage about 3/16" diameter used for tying and wrapping objects, now seldom seen.

Maynard, Walter: Lived on Potter Court. My friend and swordfishing companion. After my Dad, he had the sharpest eyes for finning swordfish of all the men I fished with. Unfortunately, he passed away in 1994.

McInnes, Walter: World famous naval architect, designed many commercial fishermen ranging in size from 25 ft to 100. His son, Alan, continues the family tradition.

Morgan, Agustus V.: Brother of Wayland Morgan, a Baptist Deacon, Mrs. Goodman's second husband and at one time my Dad's legal guardian. Lived in Giblin's house off Chesebro Avenue.

Morgan, Wayland: Brother to Augustus Morgan. Boatbuilder and clever tinkerer. Lived on the waterfront in the last house on the right on Chesebro Avenue now owned by the Woods.

On the Hook: At anchor.

Overhead Rig: Formerly a common arrangement on "Western Rigged" trawlers whereby the trawl wires were run through blocks suspended overhead between the mast and the boom.

Palmer, Nathaniel B. (1799-1877): Sealer, explorer, early clipper ship designer, trader to the Orient. Probably Stonington's best known mariner. Captain of the 44 ft sloop HERO when he discovered Antartica at 21 years of age on his 3rd voyage to the sealing grounds off Cape Horn. The Palmer Peninsula in Antartica was named in his honor.

Palmer Shipyard: Once the largest builder of wooden vessels between Boston and New York. Now the site of Noank Shipyard.

Parceling: Wrapping a rope to protect it against chafe, usually with burlap or canvass.

Pelagic: Generally, oceanic migratory fish such as swordfish and the tunas.

Pennant: To a yachtsman, a narrow flag. Colloquially to a fisherman, a short length of line attaching a bouy or lobster pot to the main warp.

Quirk Island: The middle of the two small Islands to the northeast of Ram Island off Noank.

Race, The: The Race is the area between Race Rock Lighthouse and Little Gull Island. In early colonial times it was referred to as the "Horse Race" due to the swift current. This is especially true on the ebb when it can run in excess of 5 knots at Perigee and New Moon tides. The 300 ft deep trench between Race Rock and the 20 to 30 ft shoal at Valiant Rock is one of the most productive lobster grounds in Southern New England, but the deep water, combined with the swift current streaming through the area, causes the lobster buoys to be sucked underwater for all but about an hour on each side of the slack. This, in turn, requires the lobstermen to work at top speed in order to maximize the number of pots they are able to haul before the current drives the buoys under again.

Ram Island: Original (and current) name for the 16 acre island off Noank. Previously called Mystic Island for many years.

Ram Point: Low gravel point on the northwest corner of Masons Island.

Reynolds, Dr. Robert: A Hartford orthopedic surgeon and one of my Dad's best customers. Performed the amputation of my Dad's cancerous leg and continued to monitor his condition until the end.

Rockaway: Manufacturer of high-quality fishing chairs. Once the industry standard which others were measured against.

Rube Goldberg: American cartoonist Ruben Goldberg who specialized in portraying very complicated, improvised mechanical gadgets.

Ryley, Dr. Roger: Mystic General Practitioner. Our family doctor, a close friend of the entire family and one of the finest human beings I have ever known. Lived originally on Gravel Street, then aboard his beloved Penbo Trawler at Cottrell's Dock for many years before moving ashore in his old age. He came every day to administer morphine when my Dad was in terminal care. They just don't make them like that any more.